AF407145

*From Unimaginable Loss
to Rewritten Grief,
Find the Life Waiting for You*

I Carry You

Christina Stiverson

I Carry You: From Unimaginable Loss to Rewritten Grief, Find the Life Waiting for You © Copyright 2025 by Christina Stiverson

All rights reserved. No part of this publication may be reproduced, distributed or transmitted in any form or by any means, including photocopying, recording, or other electronic or mechanical methods, without the prior written permission of the publisher, except in the case of brief quotations embodied in critical reviews and certain other noncommercial uses permitted by copyright law.

Although the author and publisher have made every effort to ensure that the information in this book was correct at press time, the author and publisher do not assume and hereby disclaim any liability to any party for any loss, damage, or disruption caused by errors or omissions, whether such errors or omissions result from negligence, accident, or any other cause.

Adherence to all applicable laws and regulations, including international, federal, state, and local governing professional licensing, business practices, advertising, and all other aspects of doing business in the US, Canada, or any other jurisdiction, is the sole responsibility of the reader and consumer.

Neither the author nor the publisher assumes any responsibility or liability whatsoever on behalf of the consumer or reader of this material. Any perceived slight of any individual or organization is purely unintentional.

The resources in this book are provided for informational purposes only and should not be used to replace the specialized training and professional judgment of a health care or mental health care professional.

Neither the author nor the publisher can be held responsible for the use of the information provided within this book. Please always consult a trained professional before making any decision regarding treatment of yourself or others.

For more information, email christina@graduategrief.com.

ISBN: 979-8-9949979-0-1 – Ebook
ISBN: 979-8-9949979-1-8 – Paperback
ISBN: 979-8-9949979-2-5 – Hardcover

My Invitation to You

There was a time I believed I might never fully live again. I felt like my world ended the day my daughter died, and the years since have been an unraveling and a rebuilding all at once.
I share my story here because I hope it might be the mirror you need, and the map you have been searching for.

I believe that grief can be rewritten,
even when the path seems impossible to see.

If you are seeking connection and gentle reminders that healing is still possible, I would be honored to welcome you into my community where I share tools, stories, and glimpses of hope for the days when you feel lost.

And if, by the time you reach the end of this book, you feel ready to transform and begin rewriting your own grief, I have created *The Rewritten Pathway Reflection Guide*—a free workbook and journal drawn from the seven steps I share in these pages. It is waiting for you whenever you are ready to take the first step.

Until then, in the space between grief and possibility—
I Carry You.

Join me at graduategrief.com.

Beyond These Pages

A portion of the proceeds from this book will be donated to the Foundation for Addie's Research. On average in the United States, over forty children per day are diagnosed with cancer, and they deserve to have people fighting for them.

We are working tirelessly to create more options for children like Addie, helping to discover treatments that are less toxic and more effective against this rare disease. By reading these pages, you help carry her story forward and bring us closer to that day.

Thank you for standing with us and for believing in a future where these children have more tomorrows. For more information, please visit: addiesresearch.org

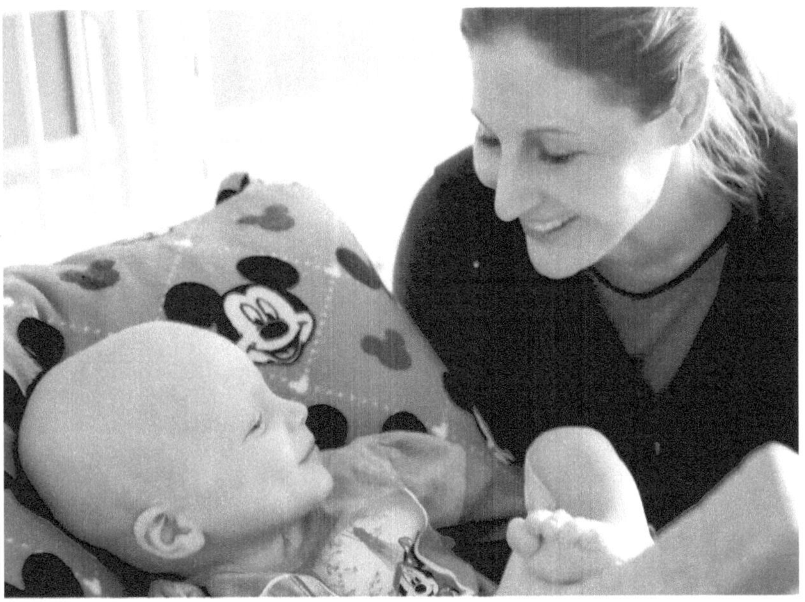

Photo Credit: Flashes of Hope, Lynn Townsend

Contents

Foreword — 9

Prologue — 13

1. Small but Mighty — 15
2. Edge of Insanity — 31
3. The Things We Carried — 43
4. Anatomy of Waiting — 57
5. Chasing Hope — 71
6. The Gift of Moments — 81
7. Life with the Windows Down — 95
8. It's OK to Not Be OK — 111
9. The Year that Wasn't — 123
10. Questions to the Universe — 151
11. To Be Unbroken — 169
12. Evolution of a Miracle — 187
13. Rewritten Pathway — 203

Step 1: Recover — 205
Step 2: Endure — 209
Step 3: Wonder — 213
Step 4: Reframe — 219
Step 5: Integrate — 225
Step 6: Transform — 229
Step 7: Evolve — 233

Epilogue — 237

A Final Note — 239

Acknowledgements — 241

References — 247

About the Author — 249

Foreword

Dear Reader,

Before the first page of this book was ever written, a little girl changed us all. Her name was Adelaide, and we will always call her Addie.

This story is deeply personal. It's not only a story about loss, it's a story about love—the fierce, transcendent kind that reaches across generations and binds a family together through the worst kind of heartbreak.

I am Christina's mother. And I am Addie's grandmother.

Four days before Addie's second birthday, we received *the* call, the moment that our world split into "before" and "after." I was walking down the stairs in our New York home when I picked up the phone.

"We are being transported to Children's Hospital Colorado," Christina said. "The doctor found a large tumor in Addie's liver. She says it's cancer." Within twenty-four hours, my husband and I were on a plane, and nothing was ever the same.

We didn't go back. We couldn't. For thirteen months, our only compass was Addie. Her care, her comfort, and her beautiful life became ours too. Christina and her husband were experiencing the unimaginable. We did what we could to help by taking care of Addie's baby sister and quietly trying to carry the weight no one should ever have to bear alone.

There's something unique about a grandparent's love. It's deep, joyful, and all-encompassing. It's hard to put into words until you have felt it. A grandmother's heart has two layers. One layer broke as I watched Addie endure treatment—so small and impossibly strong. I would have taken her place in an instant. The second layer broke as I watched my daughter fight with every ounce of her being to save her child while hiding her raw agony.

And then, we lost her.

The grief was indescribable. That kind of sorrow that rips through the soul. And yet, life went on. My daughter was still here, but without her first-born child. *Would she be able to survive this? Would her marriage endure? Would I lose her too?*

Christina didn't grieve the way I expected. She held it inside. She didn't want to be pitied or comforted. And I had to respect that, even when it hurt. As her mother, however, that left me questioning: *How do I show up without stepping in too far? How do I support her without trying to fix something I couldn't possibly fix?* I longed for us to cry together, to say out loud what we were both feeling, hoping the tears could wash away the awful ache. But she needed time, so I waited.

We left our family roots—and our house of forty years—behind to be close to her, first in borrowed space, then in a motorhome, then temporary apartments. Eventually, we bought a house in Colorado only ten minutes away. That was the sudden realization that the move would be permanent. However, the day we signed the papers, my father went into the hospital. Three weeks later, he was gone. My mother was left alone in New York. More loss. More grief. More decisions. And still, we stayed, ready for what came next. Because this was where we were meant to be.

Over time, I watched my daughter begin to rise. I watched her rebuild by moving forward and carrying Addie with her. She created a foundation in Addie's name. She built a network to support other families. She spoke and gave back to her community. And one day, she told me something I will never forget. She had learned to reimagine her unbearable pain and truly value her life again.

That was the moment something changed in me. The weight in my heart became lighter. We started talking, really talking, about the things we hadn't been able to say before. And I realized: my daughter was not only healing, but she was lighting the way for others.

This book is part of that light.

It is raw. It is honest. It is full of the kind of truth that only comes from walking through fire. But it's also full of something even more powerful: hope. If you've lost someone, if you've ever wondered how to keep breathing through unthinkable loss, Christina's story will help you feel less alone. She offers you a hand to hold.

These pages contain things she never said aloud. Things that helped me understand my own grief. Things that helped me heal and can help you too.

This book is for anyone who has felt like they might never feel joy again. For the parent who lost a child, the spouse who lost a partner, and the person who lost themselves along the way. This book is for the one still showing up while their heart is shattered. For the one who does not want to suffer anymore, but does not know how to stop. It is for the person staring at their own story, wondering if it can be rewritten.

It can, and Christina shows you how.

Grief will always be part of you. It will shift and evolve. It will feel quieter some days, and louder others. But you are not meant to suffer forever. That is not your destiny.

So I invite you to open your heart to this book. To Addie's legacy. To a mother's courageous grief journey. To the story of how, even in the deepest darkness, love finds a way to shine through and lift us up.

Christina, I am profoundly proud of you. This story is a gift. Thank you for offering it so bravely to the world.

With all my heart,

Linda

Prologue

I can still feel the desperate chill that filled the air when the strikingly pregnant doctor carefully re-entered the treatment room.

The overhead lighting was blinding, but my daughter was resting peacefully in my arms for the first time in days. Her tiny frame, thirty-three inches tall and twenty-two pounds in weight, was curled up on my lap like a snail tucked in its shell, and my father-in-law sat nervously by my side. His hands were shaking, and his breath was so deep I could see his chest rise and fall. I'm sure he had pondered the severity of the situation, but my mind was completely devoid of any thoughts besides physically comforting my daughter at that moment.

And just like that, it happened. The beautiful, glowing, pregnant doctor told me my daughter had a rare childhood liver cancer that I could not even pronounce.

Time stood completely and utterly still; my body was paralyzed. She explained she was reasonably certain of the type based on imaging and the ultrasound, but her voice became mute to me. Hearing the word "cancer" and my child's name in the same sentence was like having a tornado touch down right in front of me.

The shockwave of emotion was so intense, I could have fallen over from the weight of a feather grazing my sleeve. My father-in-law was a thyroid cancer survivor, but I had never known anyone personally whose child had cancer.

To be frank, I just hadn't been paying attention. At that moment, I was struck by the realization that a child could even get cancer. But since that day, I have seen more movies with a childhood cancer reference than I could even imagine—never mind the St. Jude commercials that haunt me in my sleep.

I had been living in my blissful baby bubble until my world came crashing down. My daughter had cancer. And my life was changed, *forever.*

1

Small but Mighty

"Everything you want is on the other side of fear."

—Jack Canfield

I have never been one to follow the path set before me. I was always too busy carving my own. From the time I was little, I was strong willed, tenacious, and had more energy than my parents knew what to do with. Whether it was protesting bedtime with the passion of a mini revolution or skipping jacketless into the New York winter, determined to prove frostbite was a myth, I was unshakable. Rules were suggestions at best, obstacles at worst. My parents learned quickly that logic rarely stood a chance against my resolve and relentless spirit.

Growing up, tiny battles were my training ground. I balked at going to church, eating anything green, or staying in my room when grounded. Each victory felt like a stake planted deeper into the world I was determined to claim. Even then, before I knew real hardship, I somehow understood that stubbornness would be both my shield and my sword.

When I was three years old—pure motion and mischief—my mind spun as fast as my feet, always chasing something just out of reach. One day in our living room, I was racing across the floor on my Mr. Lion toy, pushing with one foot and hopping on mid-roll. But the wheels caught, and when I jumped on, I bit down so hard on my tongue it nearly sliced off. My mom said it was hanging by a thread. The surgeon warned I might never speak again. Somehow, they stitched it back together. My mom called it a miracle. I didn't understand then, but now I do.

My body healed, but I never did learn to slow down. There was something in me, wild and wired, that kept pushing forward—no matter the cost. It would take decades before I understood what my brain had been trying to tell me all along. But even back then, I think I knew: I wasn't meant for the easy road, I was meant to survive.

My built-in best friend and partner in crime, my brother Greg, was just eighteen months behind me, but always towering over me like a giant. We were thick as thieves, drawn together by the unspoken understanding that siblings sometimes knew each other better than anyone else ever would. Our bond was sealed, not by words, but by scraped knees, family trips, and the quiet loyalty of growing up side by side.

Greg had always had a talent for defying gravity. As a kid, he would leap off our two-story roof into the pool or go flying down steep sledding hills, building speed, only to catch air off a jump he had carved out of snow. He was fearless in the air in a way I admired, destined to fly before he ever became a pilot.

As a third-generation Italian-American, family and carbohydrates ruled my universe, and gymnastics became my refuge from a young age. By junior high school, I looked like a college gymnast. The sport demanded everything I had, physically and mentally, and in return, it gave me something that would carry me through every challenge to come: grit.

By the time I graduated high school in 1997, my thirst for adventure burned so fiercely that staying still felt like suffocation. I packed my bags and left New York for the rugged mountains of Colorado. There I studied architecture, joined the Air Force ROTC, and spotted a brochure that I could not look away from: "Join us for the toughest workout around."

I was sold. Practices began at 4:30 a.m. at a tiny reservoir that was frigid and silent most mornings. I rowed my first year and became a coxswain the next, coaching and strategizing for a sport clearly designed for people with legs twice as long as mine, but I loved it. I craved the discipline, the crisp air entering my lungs, and the rhythm of oars slicing through water in the dark.

Rowing was a passion I found, but military service was a long held desire. I had known from a young age that I wanted to serve in the military just like my dad. After college, I began my Air Force career: commanding officer by day, fitness instructor by night, and eternal overachiever—I was stacking night classes on top of it all. I was a firecracker, fueled by pure willpower and a playlist of heart-pounding music.

The idea of slowing down was laughable. Yoga? Meditation? Those were words for other people. I needed mountains to climb, literally and figuratively, to keep the fire inside me from consuming itself.

And climb I did. By the time I was thirty-three, I had stood at the top of peaks on every continent. But each summit was a placeholder, a promise to myself that one day, I would exchange crampons and ice axes for diaper bags and bedtime stories.

Motherhood was never a question for me. It was something I always wanted, a quiet thread woven through every season of my life.

But getting pregnant in my mid-thirties was not the fairytale I'd hoped for. It was a hustle, a meticulous operation of calendars, thermometers, and timing that required every ounce of energy, patience, and hope I had. It became a second full-time job, one I clocked into with the same determination I once used to have with sports and mountain climbing.

Nothing worth having ever came easy—that truth was etched into my bones long ago. Each time I took a pregnancy test, my heart pounded harder than at any finish line I had ever reached. When the test finally turned positive, I was overwhelmed by a cocktail of surprise, relief, and sheer gratitude. Being a mother would be the most important job of my life, and that job was finally beginning.

Pregnancy, though, was not my shining season. I always admired women who glowed through those nine months, speaking lovingly about their expanding bellies and the miracle of life. I was not one of them. Carrying a watermelon-sized human inside my four-foot-eleven frame was far less poetic. My mind, trained for endurance and strength, fought this transformation like a stubborn mule. I ached. I swelled. I despised the feeling of losing control over the one thing I had always trusted: my physical body.

When we found out we were having a girl, the joy I felt made all the discomfort worth it. I pictured bows, ruffled dresses, and tiny ballet slippers—a fantasy far removed from my frilless tomboy childhood. Funny how life catches you off guard like that sometimes.

Every part of me, every stubborn, fiery inch, was forged for that moment.

The fear that came with childbirth felt different. It was not the kind you can talk yourself out of by tying your shoes tighter or setting a new goal. It was primal and raw. I begged my doctor for a C-section, convinced my tiny frame would not survive labor. He said it was an unnecessary surgery to plan for, and he denied my request. I imagined my baby stuck in my birth canal, helpless and trapped. I feared the pain of pushing such a delicate being so forcefully out of my small body. We spoke about medication, and I was open to the option if I needed it, but I still didn't know what to expect. The panic tightened in my chest just thinking about it, but I knew I had to deliver my baby.

It reminded me of confined space training at the fire academy years ago. We had to crawl through a tunnel no more than two feet in diameter, forty feet long, and filled with simulated smoke. It amplified one of my worst fears: being trapped.

This will be easy for you, I told myself as I waited my turn. *You are small. You will cruise through this.*

I watched six-foot men squeeze their way through, oxygen tanks strapped to their backs. When it was my turn, I charged forward with misplaced confidence, until I crawled into that tunnel. Darkness. No visible exit. My breathing spiked, shallow and desperate. My oxygen tank suddenly felt low on air and too big to fit through. Every cell in my body screamed, "You will get stuck and run out of air."

The fear was so real, so visceral, it dissolved logic into dust. I pushed one toe forward at a time, clawing my way through riveted steel with every ounce of will I had. On the outside, I was composed. Inside, I was a mess of terror and sweat. When I backed out of the tunnel with only seconds to spare on my oxygen tank, I knew I was not ready to become a firefighter. *How could I save someone else when I could barely save myself?* I left that academy with a bruised ego and a new understanding tucked deep in my heart: I was not fearless.

Now, facing childbirth, that same electric fear I felt in the tunnel wrapped around my chest.

How could I bring a life into this world if I was not certain of the process? Could I endure the pain without medication? Could my baby fit through the tiny passage in my body? Those were thoughts I didn't have answers for. And yet, if there was one thing my life had taught me, it was this: Fear does not mean you stop. It means you find a way. And trust me, I was about to find a way.

The word "hypnobirthing" sounded like a Las Vegas magic show to me: part hypnosis, part wishful thinking, and a whole lot of "I will try anything to survive childbirth without losing my mind."

I was skeptical, to say the least. But after combing through article after article, armed with a fierce desire to conquer my fear of giving birth, I decided to dive in headfirst. What did I have to lose? Besides my dignity, maybe.

My husband, Cody, and I signed up for a series of personalized hypnobirthing classes, filled with cautious optimism. As a fighter pilot in the Air Force, he'd spent years honing the ability to think clearly in the midst of chaos. While I made carefully thought-out decisions, Cody took on life as it came, a skill that never failed to impress me. That would be helpful as we embarked on our journey.

The hypnobirthing office was the kind of place you would expect to find a sage-burning, crystal-wearing guru. The air was thick with the pleasant scent of rainwater and lavender. The lighting was dim, the recliner was ruby red and looked like it had lived through a few too many clients. I wondered how often they washed that blanket, but then decided ignorance was bliss.

The sales pitch for hypnobirthing was simple: "Birthing is a natural, beautiful, painless process. You, too, can have this experience."

I wanted so desperately to believe it, even as my inner cynic rolled her eyes so hard, they nearly got stuck. Every birth scene I had ever watched in movies looked anything but painless, and one of my friends had just rehashed her torturous birth experience with me over coffee the previous day. She was in painful labor for over fifty hours, even with medication, and then she needed a C-section because she could not push the baby out. Still, I clung to the tiniest thread of hope that what was advertised was still possible.

Fear had never settled that deeply into my bones before. Not during fire academy training. Not forging to the summit of a remote mountain halfway across the world. Not solo freefall parachuting out of a perfectly good aircraft. No, childbirth felt different. It felt ominous. There was no option to back out.

I whispered to myself more times than I could count, *If teenage girls can do this, surely a grown woman with three-and-a-half decades under her belt can manage.* I had conquered my fears before with mantras of knowing that others, who I believed possessed far less mental fortitude, had been doing this for centuries. That helped me.

Cody had his doubts about my hypnobirthing plan, especially after the hypnotist casually claimed he could cure his snoring, something three nose surgeries had failed to accomplish. But he humored me, because deep down he knew I needed a lifeline to survive the biggest unknown of my life.

Wearing the only pants that still fit, I slid into the chair and closed my eyes, ready to visualize my way into a serene birth experience. Somehow, against all odds, I allowed myself to believe it. Cody sat on the sofa next to me, ready to breathe his way into zen also.

Guided by the expert's voice, I imagined myself looking out from the balcony of a beach house. Now I'm not really a beach person, and I don't love humid weather because it makes my hair frizz.

However, I didn't want to doubt the process, so I committed. It was a scene I recalled from a movie I could not remember the title of. I could hear the waves crashing below me. I could feel the thick, salty air blowing against my face. I could see the weathered but sturdy wooden staircase right in front of me.

I began to go down. Each step was slow, deliberate, and somewhat grounding. And I started to count:

Ten...*RELAX, RELAX, RELAX*. I took a deep breath in through my nose, and then blew the longest breath out possible through my mouth.

Nine...*RELAX, RELAX, RELAX*. The rhythm was steady and became a mantra to me. Step by step, I descended toward the water.

Eight...*RELAX, RELAX, RELAX*. My feet gently pressed onto the damp wood planks. I could even feel the coolness from the water.

Each number, each step down, was a small victory. I could feel an intense relaxation in my body, something I had never experienced before. I felt a sliver of confidence in the possibility that what was advertised could work for me. And then the hypnotist woke me and our session was over.

When we departed the office, grounded back in reality, Cody mentioned, "That was pretty relaxing."

I thought, *will it be enough?*

Thanksgiving in Fairbanks, Alaska, was like a scene from a winter survival movie. Temperatures plummeted to minus forty degrees, the kind of cold where boiling water thrown into the air vanishes instantly. I did not need to do that to tell me it was cold; my frozen nostrils confirmed it just fine.

At thirty-one weeks pregnant, my cantaloupe-sized torso had no more room to give, and our baby girl seemed determined to break a rib or two with her daily kickboxing matches. Each kick was a reminder that she was strong—and that my organs were not.

We had just interviewed a potential doula, but I was hesitant. She was still breastfeeding her four-year-old son. Admirable, yes, but relatable? Not for me. There was no way I'd still be breastfeeding a four-year-old. I figured if you made it a few months, you deserved five stars. I wanted someone who had similar child-rearing ideas to mine. But I was desperate enough to consider her, understanding that beggars couldn't be choosers, especially in a small town.

The final hypnobirthing class remained. This would be the session where my diligent labor visualization practice would culminate, and I would learn how to breathe through the birthing process.

That was when I noticed a little leakage.

Initially, I blew it off. Pregnant women peeing themselves is basically a rite of passage, right? But when it happened several more times, I hesitantly mentioned it to Cody. I said, "Honey, can you Google something for me, 'liquid coming out of a pregnant woman.'"

"Maybe it is amniotic fluid," he suggested, in his calm, reasonable voice—that somehow made me want to throw a pillow directly at his face. "We may need to get it checked out."

I was in full denial that anything needed to be "checked out" that evening. I still had two months to go in that pregnancy, and I was sure it was just my muscles getting weaker from the growing pelvic pressure. Cody gently reminded me that this was his baby too. *Fine.*

He won that round. We called the hospital. I was sure they'd tell us we were overreacting.

"Come in immediately," they said.

Cue my internal screaming and his snarky look.

When we arrived, I felt fine. Well, as fine as someone could feel when being internally pummeled by a tiny martial artist. I expected the doctor to send me home. Instead, she confirmed my water had indeed broken.

I was stunned. This was not how it was supposed to happen. No dramatic taxi scene. No gush of water onto the pavement like in the movies. Just a slow leak and a lot of disbelief. I was two days shy of thirty-two weeks, and we were just told the local hospital did not support babies born under thirty-two weeks. *Wait a minute. Does this mean I am going into labor now or am I just going to be put on bed rest?* I was convinced I was still two months away from giving birth, and I wanted to go home.

Despite my protest that we did not need to be flown to a larger city nearly 350 miles away, they scheduled the flight and told me we were leaving in just over an hour. My fear of giving birth was now being taken on an involuntary road trip. Apparently someone knew something I didn't.

We were still weeks away from packing the famous "hospital go-bag." You know, the one with the lavender essential oils, the "going home" outfit for the baby, the giant padded underwear, and the fancy purple hospital gown I convinced myself would make post-birth photos look glamorous. None of it was packed yet.

Cody sprinted home to grab whatever he could find while our kind neighbors, bless their hearts, rummaged through our closets, tossing clothes into a suitcase. Desperate times called for desperate measures, and desperate measures apparently included two retired Alaskans packing my delicates.

Oh, and in case you are wondering: the gown, the baby outfit, and the lavender oil did not make it.

The paramedics strapped me to a yellow plastic backboard as if I was an injured hiker plucked off a mountain. Except this mountain was called "Motherhood," and I was nowhere near the summit.

The small medevac jet barely fit the medic, Cody, and me. As the engines roared to life, I realized with grim clarity that we had not finished our hypnobirthing classes. We had not hired the doula, and I had no idea what contractions would actually feel like.

The flight was short for Cody, but felt endless to me. Every bump, every turn, sent new jolts of pain ricocheting through my body. My back screamed in protest as the hard backboard pressed mercilessly into my spine. I tried to joke to myself that maybe this was just an "extreme" version of labor training. The pain was sharp, deep, and relentless. Later, I would realize this was my first introduction to back labor, and it was no joke.

When we finally touched down in Anchorage just before midnight, I was whisked into the hospital. "One, two, three, lift." I heard them say to keep my body straight when they moved me from the backboard to the hospital bed. I felt paralyzed after my experience.

And just like that, my contractions stopped.

"Just hang tight for a while," the new doctor said casually, as if my mind was not spinning into a full-blown panic.

"If you do not go into labor in the next few days, we will induce you," she added.

My brain reeled. I was supposed to have eight more weeks. I didn't know anything about having a preemie. That was not mentioned in my birth plan.

But here I was.

Staring at the fluorescent lights of a hospital ceiling. Waiting. Wondering how long I would be in that room and if I had any idea what I had gotten myself into.

Early the next morning, on December 3rd, 2013, I went into full-on labor. I began to shake uncontrollably. I was not exactly sure if this was labor or if I was having a convulsion. I was rushed to the delivery room.

The pelvic pain was unrelenting, my legs were stiff, and my body felt out of my control. As the contractions grew stronger, I fought to breathe calmly. I tried to relax and needed to focus. My hypnobirthing training had been months in the making, but the fact that our baby was coming almost two months early and we had not finished the classes made me scared.

I recalled the techniques: the visualization, the relaxing breaths, and the countdown. I closed my eyes and imagined myself stepping down the wooden staircase from the beach house. I started to count down like I had practiced.

Still, my fear was sharp and gnawing, as were the contractions. I could hear the distant panic in the back of my mind, urging me to ask for medication. I wanted the pain to stop, but I also wanted to prove that I could do it using the natural breathing techniques I had learned. I had prepared for this, even if I hadn't practiced enough. I decided to push through on my own.

Each number, each step down, was a small victory. I could make it. Slowly, the fear began to fade, replaced by intense focus and quiet determination. I would start at the top of the stairs again when I got to one, never letting my feet touch the sand, because I knew I needed to keep going. The repetition became my anchor, a lifeline in the chaos of my body.

I had no idea what was happening in the room around me. I was deep in my hypnotic trance. Cody later told me, "You seemed like you were on another planet." Occasionally, my visualization would break, and I would hear the doctor giving me cues to bear down and breathe forcefully through a contraction. I tried desperately to follow her orders, but felt confused in those moments. I didn't get to attend the last class.

I turned to Cody as he stood by my side, calm as ever. "Chris, I know exactly how you need to breathe. Let me help you," he said. "This is just like pulling Gs in the F-15."

His words made some sense. After all, he'd been trained to endure pressure. But in the moment, they were just surreal and annoying. I wanted to argue so badly with him, to scream out, "You have no idea in hell what this is like," but I didn't. My body and mind fought that primal instinct. I needed his calmness, his certainty, just as much as I needed to feel my own breath.

I could hear faintly in the background, "We can't find the baby's heartbeat with the monitor anymore. She needs to get this baby out quickly," and that's when my body took over. It did what it needed to do, despite my lack of training. I pushed through the pain I had feared so deeply and delivered her naturally. I heard her cry just briefly, and a rush of relief came over me. She didn't get stuck.

Finally, I was able to hold her in my arms. I had done it and I was proud of myself. But my moment of peace was fleeting. My body was still reeling from the intensity of it all and I began to tremble.

There was happiness, yes, but there was also a feeling that this wasn't finished yet, that the journey was not over. There was a pause, a quiet before the storm that I couldn't quite explain. I held her for only a few seconds, barely enough time to memorize the curve of her cheeks, before the nurse swept her away and passed her through something similar to a pharmacy window.

And as I looked down at my empty arms, my heart swelled with confusion and a strange apprehension. I knew that the next chapter had only just begun.

She was a warrior from the beginning.

We named her Adelaide, after a remote island off the Antarctic Peninsula where Cody and I spent our honeymoon. It reminded us of our once-in-a-lifetime experience—the kind you splurge on because you crave exploration and adventure. Years later, I discovered Adelaide meant "the noble one." It fit her perfectly. Even as a newborn, she carried a fierce strength that seemed far bigger than her tiny frame.

I also won the nickname battle, a victory that gave me a true sense of satisfaction. Cody had been against nicknames, but after growing and birthing an actual human, I felt entitled to a small win. So, Adelaide Marie became Addie, a name sweet enough for a child, strong enough for a woman.

She weighed four pounds, six ounces, and measured seventeen inches long—delicate as a whisper but tougher than she looked.

I told Cody to follow our baby where they were taking her and I would "finish up." I had done it. I survived childbirth, without any medication, with all the intensity and pain and pride that comes with it.

It was over.

And then, the doctor reached into my body and ripped the placenta from the wall of my uterus—which felt like torture straight out of the depths of hell.

Welcome to motherhood, I thought.

Walking into the NICU was like stepping onto another planet, one where time moved differently and hope flickered. Rooms with incubators were all around us; tiny lives suspended between fight and fragility. Some babies were even smaller than Addie, their skin almost translucent, their futures uncertain.

The air was thick with quiet urgency, the soft beeping of machines the only constant sound. Parents whispered prayers in sterile corners. Nurses moved with a quiet presence, gentle in their care but swift in their actions. It was a world no parent dreamed of entering, yet here we were.

Addie was jaundiced, her skin tinted a deep yellow. Her liver, still developing, struggled to do its job. She spent most of her early days under special lights, wearing a tiny eye mask that made her look like a pint-sized superhero. We took a picture of her lying there, one hand raised, and titled it "follow me to freedom" in our photo book. Even then, Addie seemed to possess an ancient wisdom, as if she knew the road ahead would not be easy, but she was ready to lead the way.

We barely got to hold her—each precious minute we could was rationed more carefully than gold. Every touch, every whispered promise, we were stitching a piece of ourselves to her fragile body. We dressed her in doll clothes because even the preemie size was too big. This was our first taste of reality, and any and all concerns we had about caring for our little being were validated.

Somehow, miraculously, we were cleared to leave the hospital in record time. The nurse originally told us we should plan to stay several weeks, even months. However, each day Addie met one more requirement on the discharge checklist. She learned to eat well and grew big enough to fit safely in a car seat. Her bilirubin levels kept getting better and her color improved.

Fifteen days later, we boarded an Alaska Airlines flight, half cargo, half passengers. Addie was nestled against me in a soft pink baby sling, hardly bigger than a loaf of bread. I soaked up every curious glance, every double-take from strangers who could not believe such a tiny being was tucked safely against my chest. It felt good to be seen as a mother. I finally felt that glow that I never knew during pregnancy.

When we walked into our house a week before Christmas, the dishes from Thanksgiving were still drying in the rack, a time capsule of a life that had changed forever. Addie came home nearly six weeks before her due date, defying every odd stacked against her. We celebrated with joy and gratitude. We cherished that Christmas deeply.

I had survived my pregnancy, the raw fear of childbirth, the chaos of a medical evacuation, the unknown status of how hypnobirthing could help me, and the balance of NICU life. I thought the hardest part was behind us; but life was only beginning its lesson on perseverance.

Dear Addie, thank you for ... making me a mother, one of my greatest joys in life, and giving me the strength I never knew I had.

2

Edge of Insanity

*"We are all apprentices in a craft where
no one ever becomes a master."*

—Ernest Hemingway

Two years passed quickly, and before we knew it, we had *two* beautiful girls. Amelia, whom we called Mili, was six months old—her name was a tribute to Amelia Earhart and the life of flying Cody and I had built. On the surface, everything looked just as it should. Two little girls, a loving marriage, a life filled with all the ordinary joys and struggles.

Underneath, though, something was slipping through the seams. Something I could not name.

We had a trip planned to Colorado—we'd leave the day after Thanksgiving to visit Cody's family. For months leading up to our trip, Addie was not herself. She endured fevers that came and went, along with vomiting and exhaustion. I dragged her to the doctor on the military base more times than I could count, feeling utterly deranged, only to be reassured with phrases such as, "just teething" and "a simple stomach bug." I demanded a blood test, something, anything to prove I was not losing my mind. Our doctor prescribed iron supplements, which I soon learned were twice the normal dose for a toddler.

My blood began to boil; I questioned everything. Each visit left me raw. I brought Cody along for reinforcement, desperate for validation that I was not imagining things. We even landed in the emergency room several times, but the answer was always the same: "Nothing to worry about." I was screaming inside for someone to listen. Fear clawed at my insides as I spiraled into endless Dr. Google searches late at night, convincing myself of a thousand diagnoses.

Am I one of those crazy paranoid moms? I wondered briefly, then shut down that thought. This was more than a passing virus. I felt it.

It built and built until Thanksgiving Day 2015, when my spirit finally cracked. Surrounded by friends in their cozy Alaskan home, I collapsed into tears—a messy, gasping release of terror and frustration. I cried in fear of the unknown, and confusion fed my outrage. Cody witnessed my meltdown and assured me he felt puzzled by her symptoms himself, but neither of us knew what to do. No amount of mashed potatoes or pumpkin pie could patch the gaping hole of desperation in my chest. I felt like a turtle in a glass tank, frantically pressing against invisible walls, screaming for help no one could hear. Not even Cody.

We arrived in Colorado the day after. We decided to celebrate Addie's second birthday a few days early—just a small gathering with cake and close family before Cody left for a planned pilot upgrade training in Oklahoma the next day.

Addie wasn't eating much and felt tired. "I'm worried something is really wrong," I said to Cody.

"I'm sure she's jet lagged from traveling," he said. "I have already postponed this training once and I need to go this time."

He kissed my forehead and, while bracing my shoulders, he whispered, "She's going to be OK. We'll figure it out." Then the girls and I curled up in his arms for the biggest family hug we had ever done. He waved goodbye smiling from the window of his parents' car as he headed to the airport.

I held my breath that day, sensing that something was about to give.

It did.

The next morning, Addie's condition worsened and I was steadfast in finding answers. I could not get her fever down and she was vomiting bile. Panic rising in my chest, I rushed her to the children's hospital satellite campus. The doctor—heavily pregnant and radiating an unspoken understanding, listened.

I sat there, clutching my daughter in my arms like a shield against the world, and said, "Something is wrong. I know it in my bones. This is not teething. This is not a virus. Please do not send us home again." My voice trembled, not from weakness, but from holding in too much for too long.

She met my stare without blinking. She nodded, her hand resting just above her belly. "I believe you," she said. "We are going to figure this out."

And in that moment, the ground beneath me steadied just enough to breathe. Instead of shrugging me off, she ordered tests, contacted infection control, and dug into the mystery with urgency. I felt as if she heard my heart screaming. I knew she would not give up till she found the answer.

And then it happened. A diagnosis. The doctor told us that Addie had a tumor the size of a grapefruit inside her liver.

The doctor found it during her physical exam, her fingers pressing gently against the Buddha belly I had always brushed off as "normal toddler belly." I recall mentioning many times to Cody that her tummy looked bigger after dinner when we would give her a bath, but I chalked it up to delicious mac-n-cheese and bloating. An avalanche of shame buried me as my hand felt the tumor in her stomach. How had I not felt it before?

Just weeks before, Addie had her two-year checkup. Her doctor had not even palpated her abdomen. At that checkup, I had cried out for help, and nobody took it seriously. Did I not fight hard enough? Did I not scream loudly enough?

Our daughter was one in a million. I had always felt that way about her, but now it was a clinical reality. Confirmed by an ultrasound of the tumor, it was Hepatoblastoma. I could not even pronounce it at first. The word itself sounded foreign and cruel. My internet searches turned into a frantic kindergarten-level spelling game as I tried to explain it to Cody over the phone.

"Only about one hundred cases per year in the United States," I told him, my voice cracking under the weight of disbelief. "This is rare and terrifying."

There was a pause. A long, aching pause.

Then he said, "One hundred? That's nothing. How the hell is this happening to us?" His voice sounded different. Strained. He was trying to process it with the same tactical calm he used in combat, but the words did not come with training for this. "I'll be there as fast as I can."

Cody rented a car and drove nine hours overnight from Oklahoma, speeding endlessly without getting a single ticket. Meanwhile, Addie and I were transported by ambulance to Children's Hospital Colorado in Aurora. I remember thinking the ambulance was overkill. She was not dying, was she? That's when the neurons in my brain started firing, and I began to crack the surface of what we might be dealing with.

My dear friend, Ashlie, a college and military friend, rushed to my side, her presence a lifeline until Cody could get there. That night, our world shifted permanently. We stood at the beginning of a journey that would demand more strength, more courage, and more heartbreak than we could fathom.

When she arrived, I did not need to explain. She took one look at me—at Addie lying in the crib with an IV in her tiny arm—and her expression cracked.

"I left as soon as I got your message," she said, setting her purse on the floor with shaking hands and tears welling up in her eyes. "I still cannot believe this is real," she whispered. "I didn't even tell anyone at work why. I just left."

I nodded slowly. "I keep hoping someone will come in and tell me they made a mistake. That it is something else. Anything else."

"I do not know what to say," she said. "But I am here."

"Thank you," I replied, staring at the monitor blinking steadily beside Addie.

Ashlie walked up next to me. She didn't try to fix it. She didn't try to offer hope or logic or statistics. And in that moment, we stood in a room that felt far too big for the size of my daughter's body and far too small for the weight of what had just happened.

Dear Addie, thank you for ... sending me a sign that you were not OK, and I was not crazy.

Addie started her first round of chemotherapy, administered through her newly implanted power port, two days before her second birthday.

There was still a mecca of unidentified details that we craved, but before we could catch our breath, she received a chemo cocktail of four different drugs. This happened even before the biopsy results were confirmed. They wanted to move quickly based on her extremely high Alpha-fetoprotein (AFP) count, a number which meant the cancer was aggressive.

The pace was dizzying. There was no time to digest or grieve. We were told to wear rubber gloves when changing her diaper for forty-eight hours afterward because the substance was so toxic. If it could burn me after she vacated it from her body, what was it doing to her insides? But I couldn't stop to think about that. The only thought that carried me through was annihilating the cancer at all costs.

On December 3rd, Addie turned two-years-old.

Balloons hovered above her hospital crib, casting soft shadows on the walls. I allowed myself a glimpse of celebration. A year ago, we threw a neighborhood party in Alaska, complete with fireworks, because in December it's dark enough to see them during the day. It was probably more for me to say, *Hey, you made it,* rather than seeing my one-year-old eat cake for the first time. That party had felt like a milestone, a joyful exhale. But this birthday felt like holding my breath under water.

Family and friends flooded us with stuffed animals and messages of love, but none of it could comfort the feeling at my core. I imagined the devastation if the doctor had told me *I* had cancer. That would have been a dagger through my heart, of course. But hearing it about my child? That was an *obliteration.*

Still dazed, we met with the oncology team. They confirmed it: Stage III Hepatoblastoma.

I knew that Stage IV was the worst, but I had to Google what the stages even meant. Stage III sounded only marginally less fatal to me. In our case, the doctor explained that she was considered Stage III because there was no metastasis detected and it was inoperable.

There was no manual to prepare me for this. No amount of military training could arm me against the fear now embedded in my bones.

"Out of all the rare liver cancers your child could have," our doctor said, "this is the one you would want. It has about an eighty percent survival rate."

When you know nothing about childhood cancer, four out of five is a lifeline with promising odds.

Our doctor said, "Most general physicians will never see a case of childhood cancer in their entire careers." Even he had seen fewer than one case per year of Hepatoblastoma—but he had worked on it before, many times in his thirty years. This fact offered a sliver of comfort, a thread of trust to cling to. Still, I understood then how easily Addie's illness had slipped through the cracks.

When our young pediatrician from Alaska called to express her sympathy, I could hear it in her voice before she even said a word. A fragile inhale. A pause. The kind of silence that swallows courage.

"I just found out," she began. "I can't stop thinking about it. I'm ... I'm so sorry."

I stood there in the hallway, phone pressed to my cheek, straddling two worlds—the one where I still trusted people and the one where I did not.

"It's OK," I said. My voice was level, but my chest was a hurricane. "We're where we need to be now. That's all that matters."

But it was not OK.

I pictured her alone in the clinic, her hands probably shaking. Maybe she would carry this moment with her forever. I already knew I would.

When I hung up, Cody stood near the sink, arms folded tight across his chest. His eyes stared at me the way he did when he was trying not to say something he knew might sting.

"You let her off easy," he said right to my soul. I turned toward him, the phone still in my hand. "She was trying," I said. "I could hear the emotion in her voice."

He shook his head, his voice quiet but sharp.

"She missed it. Over and over again. And you told her it was OK."

"I didn't want to make her feel worse," I whispered.

"She's not the one who has to fight this now," he said. "We are. Addie is. And you're being sensitive to *her* feelings?"

His words were quiet, but cold. His body radiated a kind of anger that had been simmering. He wanted me to be angry too. Cody held it together for everyone else. But for me, he let it out—because he needed someone to blame. And so did I.

As I stood by her crib that night, balloons swaying gently in the sterile hospital air, I whispered to her in her sleep, "We are going to beat this."

And somehow, I believed it.

Dear Addie, thank you for ... keeping us calm when there was no calm around us.

We established residency at Cody's parents' house, in his high school bedroom, with just enough clothes for a short vacation. The room was quaint, cozy, and made me feel like we were in a bed and breakfast, except I knew the people in the photos.

Our wedding photo was on top of the dresser. Just looking at it, I could almost hear the soft hum of love songs, the same kind of cheesy tunes you'd expect in a rom-com. And that's exactly what it felt like when I met Cody.

It was at the wedding of two of our closest military friends, a classic gathering of love, laughter, and that slightly uncomfortable feeling of being the only single woman in a sea of happy couples. I was standing at the top of a balcony in a black dress I had specifically bought for this occasion. It was the kind that clung just enough to feel dressed up but not too much to make me feel like I was trying too hard.

And that's when he caught my attention. He was casually talking with some other members of the wedding party. He looked up at me and I quickly looked away, not sure if I wanted to talk or just observe from above.

But then I caught his eye, and he gave me a smile that could melt the toughest heart. Seriously, it was as if he practiced it in front of the mirror. I was smitten.

We came up with some light conversation to introduce ourselves. His intro sounded a little like this in my mind, "Nice to meet you. I'm stationed overseas, about to deploy, and totally *not* looking for a relationship. Oh, and did I mention I'm a fighter pilot?"

I could practically hear the dramatic music pause as I raised an eyebrow. Challenge accepted. He might not have been looking for love, but I definitely was, and I wasn't one to back down from a little difficulty.

Our "romantic" journey didn't follow the typical Hollywood script. We fell for each other over emails while he was deployed for nearly a year. It wasn't glamorous, but it was our love story. Almost daily, we exchanged thoughts, hopes, and dreams. I enjoyed sharing my life stories and always looked forward to reading his deepest desires, his philosophies on life, and his darkest secrets. It was an emotional tug-of-war some days. When either of us had a bad day at work, we couldn't be there to just hold each other. We could only offer our words to connect. It seemed one dimensional, but still well worth it.

As his deployment neared the end, despite all the challenges, I knew he was the one. After all, I didn't meet a charming fighter pilot on a balcony at a wedding and then spend a year writing letters just to throw it all away. So, when he finally came back, it felt like the universe hit "play" on our personal movie, and we got married.

Looking at that photo, I couldn't help but smile at how perfectly sappy our whole story was. I was so thankful that man was beside me, ready to help me survive the biggest fight of our life so far.

We removed the doors of the closet to fit a pack-n-play for Addie next to us and still have space to walk. Six-month-old Mili was not sleeping through the night, was on the verge of crawling, and the house was nowhere close to toddler-proof. There was a staircase that made me cringe, sharp corners everywhere I turned, and a mortal fear for safety that I could not shake. I could not keep my other daughter safe from cancer, but I was determined to keep this precious little human from harm any way I could.

Cody's parents prepared for our unthinkable cancer journey and rearranged their home and their lives for us. We could not look past the day we were living in, and we needed the help. It was still like a bad dream, one we could not wake up from. My parents quickly arrived from New York and were welcomed to live at my in-laws house as though it was their own, and we were grateful.

My parents never missed anything important in my life. From gymnastics meets to helping me pack my home during every military move, they were always there. They flew to Alaska to see Addie in the NICU, and they flew to Colorado this time, not for a visit, but for an undetermined amount of time.

This diagnosis devastated our entire family, and we were all in a state of survival.

Somehow, without planning or permission, we all found our places. Cody's mom folded our laundry without asking. My dad brewed coffee before anyone else was awake. We took turns holding Addie, feeding Mili in the middle of the night, and finding the right drawer for sippy cups. There was no schedule. No routine. Just devotion wrapped around chaos. I saw it in the way they looked at her. In the way they looked at us.

Love became the rhythm we lived by when nothing else made sense.

Dear Addie, thank you for ... bringing both of our families together under one roof.

3

The Things We Carried

"Tough times don't last, but tough people do."

—Robert H. Schuller

The only thing I knew about chemotherapy was what I had seen on television. And even then, it was a vague, blurred image of a bald person attached to an IV pole. I felt foolish, as if I should have known something more, anything more. Surely I had seen a movie or listened to a friend's story about their own battle with cancer, but nothing could help me grasp the reality of what was happening to us. It didn't feel real, not in the way I needed it to. I couldn't connect those distant, fragmented images with the raw, painful experience unfolding before me. I couldn't connect it to what we were going through.

It wasn't that I hadn't cared; it was just that I hadn't *really* been there, at least not in the way I should have been. I had spent so much of my life half-focused, as if I could only pay attention to things that directly affected me.

For as long as I could remember, my brain had always been in constant chaos, and my memory felt like a sieve, losing pieces of

43

my life. I had dismissed it as the fog of "mom brain" in my thirties and forties, thinking that was just what happened when you juggled so many things at once. But it was more than that. Recently, my therapist explained it to me like this: with my constant lack of focus, I wasn't creating memories of the present. My mind was always somewhere else, wandering through a million different thoughts. I was usually planning for the future or ruminating on the past. That simple explanation unlocked a floodgate of understanding. It explained so much about my childhood, about adulthood, about the life I had been living, but was never really fully living. Maybe it was why I missed the cancer.

At the ripe age of forty-five, I was diagnosed with severe Attention Deficit Hyperactivity Disorder (ADHD). I was told I developed Obsessive-Compulsive Personality Disorder (OCPD) as my consolation prize. Suddenly, things started to make sense. The shame, the confusion, the sense of being out of control–it all clicked into place. I could now understand part of why I had felt so blindsided and overwhelmed all those years ago.

But Addie's diagnosis was eight years before I had the skills and treatment, or the self-empathy. When I found out about Addie's cancer, I felt embarrassed that I had not paid more attention to that sort of thing. I was disappointed in myself. But I couldn't let myself wallow in it for too long. I quickly picked up my self-pity, tossed it aside, and charged ahead. I was determined to face what was coming, even if I had no idea what to expect.

The world of rare cancer treatment was a foreign land, paved with blood transfusions, platelet counts, and a "nadir period" that stripped

Addie's immune system to nothing. Seven to ten days post-chemo, we were told, was when she would have no defense against the world. We learned about shots to help her white blood cells recover faster, and about side effects I had never ever considered.

Her tiny frame, already fragile, began to bear the burden of the toxic medicine. Mouth sores so raw she could not eat. Diaper rashes so severe they bled. She even got an infection on the pointer finger she used to put inside her pacifier to suck on. Her pacifier was attached, by design as a WubbaNub, to her beloved Sadie, the pink elephant that went everywhere with us. I remember the day I sat cross-legged on the hospital bed, scissors trembling in my hand, cutting the enclosed part of the pacifier to protect her from herself. She stared at me, bewildered, and then gently rested her small infected finger through the leftover rubber ring, cradling Sadie against her cheek like nothing had changed.

It broke me a little more each time she adapted faster than I did.

Addie had a collection of comfort items that we packed into a backpack so big, it looked like we were setting out on an expedition. Her Mickey Mouse pillow that Cody's mom—who Addie called Jomama—had sewn by hand, mum-mum rice crackers, and her pink Crocs worn until the bottoms became slick. Her iPad, dandelion blanket, and snack size bags of Doritos were also staples. PEZ became her favorite candy after getting her first dispenser as a gift from the hospital, and we never left home without it.

Around day twelve after her first treatment, the hair loss began. It came out in strands so fine they floated before hitting the ground. I had braced myself for many things, but not this. The first wisps caught in my hand, a quiet betrayal. Addie, barely two, had only just started to grow hair in the months before diagnosis. Now, what little she had was slipping away. It was the moment cancer stopped being an invisible enemy. It became real.

We found joy in hospital wagon rides, where I pulled Addie past the giant Christmas tree in the lobby, past the hospital gift shop, and past the sixth-floor aquarium where she smiled each time she spotted the "Nemo" fish. She would press her face against the glass while her whole body quivered with excitement. Those laps around the hospital became the best part of our days. Our oncology room faced west, where the Rocky Mountains, bathed in pink and orange sunsets, stood quietly indifferent to our battles.

We had been living in the hospital for weeks now and were discharged the day before Christmas Eve. Addie curled against me in her car seat, breathing softly. I had never felt so relieved and so terrified all at once. The hospital walls, oppressive yet safe, faded behind us. We could finally leave, but the world outside was unpredictable and cruel.

My brother, Greg, his wife, Cristy, and their family flew across the country to visit for the holidays. Addie beamed with the purest light from her soul when she saw her two cousins, who were slightly older than Mili and her. For a few hours, we all lived a different life, one where children rolled together on the floor, and laughter echoed throughout the house.

Chemo had taken Addie's ability to walk. Her muscles, stripped of strength, left her wobbling. I watched her sister Mili crawl toward her, and I saw my two babies, playing on the floor together, eighteen months apart, both bald and fragile and perfect.

Our first outing was a reckless, sanitized trip to the mall. We rented a giant red plastic car cart. I always said "no" to those because I thought it was a frivolous expense, but not this time. That day, I declared it Addie's "beep beep." She gripped the sides tightly, grinning, as we found a handicap ramp and raced down with abandon. I do not know if it was for her or for me. Maybe I needed the rush more.

When we reached the Disney Store, Addie's eyes widened, sparkling for the first time in months. It felt like we had taken her to Disneyland itself.

For Christmas, Santa left *Frozen* under the tree. While watching the movie, Addie and Mili sat side by side in matching red pajamas, Mili gently stroking her sister's bald head. That night, Cody gave me a framed photo of Addie with the words "I Carry You" underneath. The phrase was born from Addie's early attempts at language, when she raised her arms to be held and said in her softest voice, "I carry you." She had no idea that those words would one day anchor us when the storms raged the hardest.

The months that followed blurred into a collage of highs and lows. Weekly tests to monitor her tumor markers kept our hearts dangling by threads. Each good number brought hope. Each bad one shattered it.

We sanitized the world before letting it touch her. Wipes across tables, restaurant chairs, even doorknobs. A trip to Casa Bonita—a quirky but historic Colorado Mexican restaurant with cliff divers, a pirate cave, and an arcade—became a battlefield of disinfected surfaces. But we didn't care. It brought her so much joy.

Facetime calls with distant family became a ritual. Hospital cafeteria food became an acquired taste. Treatment decisions became matters of weighing devastating side effects such as permanent hearing loss or organ damage.

At one point, we were forced to confront the future of her ability to have children at just two-years-old. It was a gut punch I never saw coming. That was the price of chemo.

Cody and I clashed over the future. I thought about fertility preservation, long-term organ damage, and hearing loss—how those would affect the life she would live after cancer. Cody thought about today, about getting the tumor out of her body at any cost. I could not fault him. We were both fighting the same enemy with different weapons. It was what made us a good team.

The first hearing test post-Cisplatin showed damage. Her higher frequencies were dulled. Another irreversible casualty of her fight. Years later, while editing this chapter, I would learn about a drug finally developed to protect children from this side effect. Science is a slow, tedious process, and very little research goes into pediatric cancer therapies. It's a harsh reality to swallow. Every drug we gave to Addie was developed for adult disease; they were not designed with kids in mind.

Late night shopping runs to Target meant clearing shelves of baby mum-mums and mini-Doritos bags. Those became Addie's battle rations. "Scanxiety" crept in as a new and unwelcome companion. The hours between scans and results stretched like glass under pressure, ready to shatter at the slightest touch.

We lived in hospital rooms designed for loneliness. Cody and I slept in shifts, trading the tiny sofa bed between us. I ate scraps from Addie's untouched trays. Sometimes we could not even bear to leave for a coffee break. The world outside felt too cruel.

Some days I convinced myself that children did not die from cancer. Other days I crumbled under the weight of knowing they did. One day, we asked Addie's grandparents to sit with her so we could attend a parent support group in the hospital.

The room was small and unassuming. Beige walls. A coffee pot in the corner. Tissues on every table. We sat in silence at first, the kind that feels too heavy to break. Then the first mother spoke.

Her voice was calm, almost practiced.

"My daughter was diagnosed when she was ten. She's seventeen now. We've done everything. Every trial. Every option. But the cancer always finds its way back."

Her eyes were hollow, like someone who had cried herself empty long ago.

"She's tired," the mother added. "Sometimes I think … maybe it's time to let her go."

I felt the air leave my lungs. My throat tightened, closing in on itself. *Let her go?*

I stared at her, unable to look away or say anything. Her hands were folded neatly in her lap and she was fidgeting with a ring on her finger. I wanted to scream. I wanted to shake her. I wanted to stand up and tell her she was wrong, that she had given up, that I would never, ever say those words.

Instead, I sat frozen. My heart rejected every syllable. That would not be our future. I was convinced Addie would survive. There was no room for anything else.

Well-meaning people told me to "take care of myself." Their words, though kind, bounced off me. They did not understand. A shower was not enough. A meal away was not enough. No amount of self-care could fix the hollow pit that had opened inside me.

Cody and I tried indoor skydiving one day, desperate for a moment of escape. As I floated in the wind tunnel, I felt weightless. For two minutes, I was not a cancer mom. I was just a woman remembering how to fly. But when I emerged, reality slammed back. We missed a call with her test results. Her Alpha-fetoprotein (AFP) numbers were in, and I wanted to talk with the doctor about it. By this time, we had only a basic understanding of what monitoring her AFP levels meant. It was a biomarker in her blood that often showed disease progression or regression. However, I was left with only a voicemail and no answers. I never wanted a break again.

Despite being surrounded by family, I felt an aching loneliness that seeped into my bones. Nobody could truly understand unless they had walked this path. And even then, each path was uniquely treacherous.

One day, Addie wore a Supergirl shirt a friend had sent. She scurried around the hospital corridor with a determined wobble, her bald head shining under the fluorescent lights. I knew that shirt was for me as much as it was for her—a reminder that she was fighting harder than anyone could see.

As I watched her take wobbly steps, arms stretched wide with my mom and me on either side, I felt the familiar burn of hope ignite again in my chest. Even on the worst days, Addie carried us. She carried our fears, our dreams, and our battered hearts.

It was a typical evening at our family dinner table, a cherished time when Addie was out of the hospital and we could all be together, including both sets of grandparents, under one roof. The room, filled with soft yellow light from the overhead fixture, felt warm and safe. It was the kind of place where even on the hardest days, we found a bit of comfort.

Addie had just upgraded from her high chair to a booster seat at the table. Always the curious one, she pushed her chair back slightly, bracing her feet on the edge of the table, her eyes wide open and a mischievous grin on her face.

"Addie, be careful!" I yelled with panic and concern in my voice.

Addie, flashed her contagious smile. "I'm just having fun, Mommy."

But in the blink of an eye, the chair gave way beneath her, tipping backward with a terrible, unmistakable crash. The sickening thud of her head slamming against the baseboard heater reverberated in my chest.

A second passed, one that felt like eternity. My breath was caught in my throat; for a moment, I couldn't move. Then my heart, already wearing thin from the weight of cancer and treatments, splintered into a million jagged pieces. She was on the floor, motionless.

"Addie," I tapped her aggressively, my muscle memory taking over from twenty years of CPR training. "Are you OK? Are you OK?"

I forced the words out while crying. She didn't move. I feared she went unconscious.

"Is she breathing?" I don't know who asked the question, but I felt the cold pinch of fear twist inside me as I searched Addie's face and body for any sign of life.

Then, Addie stirred. Her eyelids blinked open. "I'm OK, Mommy," she said weakly, her voice a ghost of its usual energy. But the words didn't ease my panic. How could I trust those words after everything we had already been through?

Cody was kneeling beside me now, gently cradling Addie's bald head, and then we saw the large contusion. We rushed to the ER, not knowing if it was a life-threatening injury or not. She was so fragile, everything seemed life threatening at this point.

We arrived and the bright white walls of the hospital replaced the warm, bustling ambiance of our dinner table. The reality of cancer and the constant threat hanging over our lives–it all came crashing in, heavier than any of the chaos around me. Was this it? Were we going to lose her tonight to a concussion or a brain bleed?

As we sat in that bleak ER room, Addie's small body was propped up with pillows as she calmly created a Lego tower to pass the time. It was then that I remembered, just the day before, her platelet counts had come up. That was the only thing that kept me from falling apart completely. Her blood, fragile and delicate, had been able to clot. Hours later, the doctor validated that we had narrowly escaped a catastrophic outcome.

Addie had survived this injury, but my heart couldn't help but think, *How much longer can we keep dancing on the edge like this?* The reality of this cancer journey was a constant threat. The unpredictable nature of it all was no longer something I could shield myself from. It had inched its way into our lives, relentless and undeniable.

And yet, as I held her hand that night, I couldn't stop hoping for one more day, one more family dinner.

Dear Addie, thank you for … reminding us that even in the scariest moments, love leaves a trace of light.

It was one of those beautiful winter afternoons where the sun made the snow sparkle, but there was an odd chill in the air. We walked into the doctor's office, a familiar place by now. My heart was heavy, but still held the kind of hope you only find when you've been told your child's cancer is the "best" one to fight.

As I settled in, I could almost hear the words echoing in my mind: *With the right treatment, her chances are very good. Chemo typically works, and she should be fine.* But all I could focus on was the cold and dark feeling of the room, unaffected by the sun outside.

Our oncologist, with his Santa-like rosy cheeks and usual calm demeanor, began speaking. His words, though steady, felt out of place. "The chemotherapy isn't working the way we expected–"

My heart dropped.

I blinked, hoping my ears were deceiving me. This treatment protocol was supposed to be the cure. Cancer was supposed to be a temporary detour in our life. Six months of suffering, and then we could go back to our lives. We could go back to normal. "Not working" was impossible.

Confusion ran through me, spiraling the way juice travels a looping cup straw. *How can this be?* The words kept repeating in my head, desperate for an answer that wouldn't come.

Cody's face was as pale as mine, his eyes creased with disappointment. The silence hung heavily between us, but neither of us could break it. What could we even say? The feeling of helplessness was suffocating and overwhelming. My thoughts were a tangled mess. I couldn't breathe.

Our oncologist went on, but his words were a blur. "We need to start considering other options now. A liver transplant will be something we'll have to think about."

My stomach twisted in knots and cold panic settled deep inside. *A liver transplant?* That wasn't supposed to be part of her treatment. I didn't know much about it, but I knew enough to be terrified. I knew there were risks and long-term side-effects. I knew this meant we might never be able to move back to our home in Alaska, because the kind of follow-up care required might not be supported in a small town. I wasn't ready to face it all.

At that moment, everything I thought I knew about the fight felt like it had been ripped away. This was no longer just a six-month blip in our lives. It wasn't a straightforward path to recovery. We weren't on the map anymore. We were lost.

I looked at the oncologist, searching for some shred of reassurance, but his face contained an unfamiliar uncertainty. There was something in his eyes, something I hadn't seen before—a shred of doubt with a glimpse of confusion. I wasn't imagining it.

He was as unsure as we were.

My stomach churned. For the first time, I wondered if we were in the right place. This hospital was renowned for all the latest treatments and all the resources we needed. But now we were wandering through a maze with no exit. The doctor wasn't offering us answers anymore; he wasn't sure what to do. And that felt like too much for me to carry.

I leaned over to Cody quietly and said, "Do you think we should get a second opinion?"

I couldn't ignore the nagging feeling that we weren't getting the whole picture. That we weren't talking to the expert we needed. *Where are our blind-spots?*

Cody was scared to offend our medical staff, and I was scared of hearing even worse news from multiple sources. I was scared of what it meant for our little girl. We didn't try for a second opinion that day.

As we left the office, the snow that coated the landscape outside seemed heavier. The air was frigid, and yet I felt hot and anxious, overwhelmed by everything.

We were no longer just in a fight for her life. We were in a fight for answers. And the road ahead was darker and more uncertain than I had ever imagined. Every week, as we tried new chemotherapy regimens, we saw little progress. Each failed attempt added a new layer of frustration, disbelief, and anger. The tumor didn't shrink. The chemo didn't work. And now, the liver transplant was no longer a distant possibility. It was looming closer every day.

It wasn't supposed to be like this.

Patient advocacy became the most challenging and exhausting job I had ever undertaken. Every decision—every single one—was ours to make. Cody and I were the only constants in Addie's world, and we knew her better than anyone.

But there were no easy answers now, no clear paths. There was only the fight, and the realization that our battle was far from over.

Dear Addie, thank you for … teaching me how to show up as a mom, be your best advocate, and love so deeply.

4

Anatomy of Waiting

"Legacy is not leaving something for people.
It's leaving something in people."

—Peter Strople

I never personally knew anyone who had given or received an organ. Again I was heading into unfamiliar waters.

We were ushered into a nondescript conference room for the transplant education seminar, two full days of drinking from a firehose aimed directly at our already overwhelmed hearts. A giant binder, big enough to double as an exercise weight, was handed to us with a smile that did not match the gravity of its contents. I stared at it in disbelief, thinking, *Am I supposed to read all of this? Between diaper changes and chemo appointments?*

The liver surgeon, a man whose calm demeanor bordered on eerie, began explaining what the next few months of our lives would look like. The first hundred days after transplant, he said, would be the most critical. Addie would be more vulnerable than she had ever been. The words "foreign organ" and "immunosuppressed" hovered in the air, sharp and unseen, carrying a threat I could not ignore. I scribbled notes furiously, as if writing it down could somehow make it less terrifying.

"She is status 1B," the surgeon said. "The list is regional."

I raised my hand. "How long will we wait?"

"Typically four to six weeks," he replied casually, as if we were waiting for a table at a busy restaurant.

My brain spun with questions. *What if they open her up and the tumor looks different than they expected? What if they can resect it instead—remove the tumor, leaving her liver intact? What if the new liver was not viable? What if she died in surgery?* The words whirled through my mind.

Hearing that Addie might need lifelong medication, that she could need another transplant someday, or that she could even get cancer again from the very treatments saving her, did not land. I still clung stubbornly to the vision of her running on a soccer field one day, pigtails bouncing, this whole cancer episode a distant memory.

Did you know the liver is the only organ that regenerates? It was a fun fact delivered somewhere between pages of horrifying statistics. I smiled at the irony. Of course the liver would regenerate. Of course it would be the one organ that fought back.

They delicately introduced the concept of living donors, that someone, somewhere, could voluntarily give a portion of their liver to save our daughter. I thought immediately, *I would give my liver without hesitation.* Then reality crept in, whispering doubts. It sounded simple until you realized the gravity: two major surgeries, two lives balanced on a razor's edge. *What if I did this, and something happened to me? What if I could not care for Addie and Mili afterward? Would our family survive having two patients instead of one?*

It was a brutal calculus that no parent should ever have to consider.

Sometimes, when you are drowning, a hand reaches into the water when you least expect it.

One afternoon, I took Addie and Mili to Ashlie's house for a playdate. Ashlie and I had walked parallel paths for years. We were both in the military and were both mothers navigating chaos with half-broken compasses. She was there for me the night Addie was diagnosed, and that meant the world to me.

Dan, Ashlie's husband, was not someone I had ever imagined would become part of our inner circle during that fight, but life has a way of placing people exactly where they are meant to be. He and Ashlie met on a military deployment and married the year after Cody and I. Dan had witnessed sacrifice and tragedy firsthand in service to our country, and the mark it left on him was deep and lasting. He lost his father to cancer as a boy, and now, as a father himself, our story struck a place in him that could not stay still.

As the kids played, Ashlie sat me down. Her voice trembled slightly as she spoke. "Dan and I talked," she said. "He wants to be tested. If he is a match, he wants to donate part of his liver to Addie."

The words hung in the air, a sacred offering.

How do you respond to that kind of bravery? I was stunned, honored, and deeply humbled all at once.

That was the first time I realized how profoundly other people were living our story with us. In my small private updates to family and friends, I had tried to show the reality of our days. I never imagined someone would read them and offer their own body in return.

Would I have thought of it if the roles were reversed? Would I have had the courage? The selfish part of me recoiled; could I bear the weight of feeling so indebted to a friend? What if something happened to Dan? How could I ever live with that?

The living room walls seemed to close in around me, my heart bursting with gratitude and terror in equal measure. There are some moments that brand themselves onto your soul. This was one of them.

In the weeks that followed, we waited. A whole pediatric liver would give her the best chance.

Addie blossomed in that space between. She was on a low dose of sustainment chemo; just enough to slow the cancer, but not enough to steal her sparkle. Her blood counts held steady. Her spirit soared.

We clung to normalcy as a lifeline. We went to storytime at the library, where I sometimes caught strangers' eyes lingering too long on her bald head. Some days I had the energy to smile back; other days I tucked her soft cotton hats low over her ears and pretended not to notice.

Target trips became little adventures. I let Addie pick out tiny treasures: stickers, bubbles, and the occasional pack of PEZ she insisted were "special hospital treats." Keeping busy was not just for her; it was for me too. Movement was medicine, and it was something I could control.

Every day was a bittersweet battle between savoring the moment and bracing for the next.

I kept my phone ringer at full blast, even in the dead of night, terrified we might miss "the call." I pleaded silently, hoping that her tumor was not growing faster than our donor options.

I wrote this in my journal at the time:

> The waiting time is wearing on us all. Addie knows the car route to the hospital and is now starting to express her disdain for

going. It's becoming much more difficult as she realizes more of what is going on and picks up on what we are talking about.

While we were all waiting, we celebrated three generations of March family birthdays with cake and candles, trying to stack up happy memories like sandbags against a flood. We toured the Denver Mint. We watched Mili take her first wobbly steps just before ten-months-old. Addie frequently sang "Let It Go" at the top of her lungs, serenading her stuffed animals and unsuspecting Target shoppers alike.

I marveled at her resilience, at her joy. Through it all, an unspoken clock ticked in the background. Each day she stayed healthy was a small miracle. Each day we waited was a little heavier to carry.

And yet, somehow, we found laughter. We found light. We even began to imagine a different future, tentatively exploring new military jobs and a new home closer to family. Alaska, with its wild beauty and isolation, no longer fit the fragile life we needed to rebuild.

I used to think life happened in grand, sweeping moments. Now I knew the truth; life happened in library storytimes, in stolen giggles at Target, and in cheese quesadillas. Life was tiny, defiant bursts of joy that refused to be extinguished.

Somewhere out there, a liver was waiting. We just had to hold on long enough to find it.

And then, one morning, the phone finally rang.

Dear Addie, thank you for ... revealing true friends, the depth of a human spirit, and giving me a perspective on donating life.

The phone call came at 5:21 a.m., jolting me out of a shallow, restless sleep. I did not even have to see the number. I knew. My heart began pounding so loudly I could feel it in my ears. For weeks, every call from the hospital had sent my heart racing, but this one felt different. This was *the* call.

"You have been matched with a donor. Come in immediately."

We scrambled to get dressed, adrenaline leading the charge. We left Mili, still sleeping at home, with all the grandparents living together under one roof. It was pitch black outside. I threw a jacket over my pajamas and pulled out into the dark street, heart full of hope, barely aware of anything except getting to the hospital.

Except we had ignored one crucial detail: Colorado was in the middle of a historic snowstorm.

Whiteout conditions swallowed the highway whole. Winds howled against the windshield at sixty-five miles per hour, making our borrowed SUV feel like a toy car. We crept along, peering through the swirling snow, willing ourselves forward.

When we finally arrived at the hospital, half frozen and half elated, we were greeted with devastating news: All flights in and out of the airports were canceled. Cody immediately pulled out every flight tracker he could find, his fingers scrolling his phone in a desperate search for any hope. Somewhere out there, a team was waiting to retrieve the liver that could save our daughter's life, and we were trapped in a snow globe of uncertainty.

The deceased donor, we learned, was saving several lives that day through organ donation. Teams were coordinating, battling the weather, racing against the clock. We had no information about where the organ was coming from. We knew only that it was within our region, about a two-hour flight away. We obsessed over maps, tracing possible storm paths and major cities within that radius, pretending it would help. In truth, it was the only thing keeping us from falling apart.

The hospital was hauntingly quiet. The snowstorm had shut down almost everything. Volunteers could not make it in to open the playroom, so we improvised, pulling Addie around in a red wagon through the empty halls. Her giggles echoed off the walls, a bright spark in the otherwise somber day.

Despite everything, Addie was in great spirits. She played with her toys, watched the snow fall outside the towering hospital windows, and made every nurse she met smile. Her resilience was its own kind of beauty.

Night fell, and still, no news.

Sleep that night was more of an idea than a reality. I lay on the stiff hospital sofa, staring at the ceiling, counting the minutes, feeling the weight of every second. *Will the team make it? Will the liver still be viable? Is this all slipping through our fingers? Will we now have to take Dan up on his offer?*

Morning brought a sliver of hope. The team could fly. The extraction was scheduled. We should prepare for surgery. Two more hours passed as we waited for the organ to be transported from the airport to the hospital over the icy roads. Minutes felt like hours, hours felt like lifetimes.

Addie went into surgery at 9:30 a.m. on March 25th. The procedure was projected to take eight to ten hours. I kissed her forehead, tucked her Sadie into her tiny hand, and watched as they wheeled her away under twinkling decorative lights strung above her hospital crib in her Minnie Mouse pajamas. It was a picture burned into my mind forever.

Waiting was agony. The minutes on my phone crept by. I paced the halls, peered into vending machines I had no appetite for, memorized the bland art on the walls.

A part of me still dared to hope; maybe the surgeons would find that the tumor could be removed cleanly, and they would pass the liver on to the next child waiting. But when the call came from the operating room confirming that Addie's liver was fully engulfed by the tumor, that small hope evaporated.

There was no turning back.

I called a real estate agent to prepare the paperwork to sell our house in Alaska. Meanwhile, Cody began picturing Addie's high school graduation. A new life was unfurling, one we had not chosen, but one we would embrace. We could live anywhere, as long as we were together.

Somewhere in the chaos, I found a strange comfort. My daughter was getting a new liver. She was going to make it. Through this donor alone, we found out eight families were receiving miracles all at once. I tucked that thought into my heart, a small jewel of gratitude to put next to the fear.

"The transplant went beautifully," the surgeon came out and said to us eight hours later. "Now she just needs to rest."

Seeing Addie for the first time after surgery in the Pediatric Intensive Care Unit (PICU) was like seeing her for the very first time all over again. My heart raced, my body flooded with a tidal wave of relief, and gratitude poured from every corner of my being. There she was: tiny, fierce, undeniably alive.

Addie, in true Addie fashion, was not going to sit idly in her hospital crib. Within hours, she was attempting to yank out her drain tubes and IV lines with a ferocity that startled even the seasoned nurses. They gently placed splints on her arms to keep her safe. Her mumbled, sleepy demands came soon after: her dandelion blanket, her pink Crocs, and Sadie, her faithful stuffed companion. In those small, simple requests, I found so much hope.

Her surgeon beamed with cautious optimism. The new liver was already beginning to function. They monitored it carefully with a special mechanism on her hepatic artery. She had five IV lines threading into her tiny body and a limited pain regimen, enough to take the edge off, but never too much to overwhelm her fragile new organ.

The doctors warned us the next week would be critical, monitoring for organ rejection or complications. The transplant team reminded us of the grueling hundred-day window. Addie would have two more rounds of chemo, just to make sure. Pathology would soon dissect the tumor, tell us secrets we did not yet know. The future remained a blurred canvas.

In my message to family and friends I wrote:

> Please accept our sincerest thanks for your unwavering support and for continuing to follow our family as I document the good and bad times for my own journaling need. Our heartstrings are about to be pulled even more post-surgery. The easy part is focusing on taking care of Addie, and we are extremely fortunate to have that luxury, but difficult decisions lie ahead for our work and living situation. We are still living out of a suitcase (like a bad military deployment) and have been staying in Cody's high school bedroom. The comforts of home and amazing family sacrifice have given us the perseverance and resilience we need.

But for that night, one thing was certain: Our daughter had been given another chance at life. We were relieved the transplant was done, ecstatic that the cancer-riddled liver was gone.

And somewhere beyond the hospital walls, the snow continued to fall, covering the world in a fresh, uncertain beauty.

Four days after surgery, Addie smashed all the surgical records the hospital could measure. Most children spent over a week in the PICU, but Addie already had them backing off pain meds and preparing her for a move upstairs. The high-dose steroids she endured during those first few days had temporarily turned her into a miniature toddler version of the Incredible Hulk. Her face was flushed, her energy boundless. She grunted and thrashed, desperate to escape the confines of her crib. Every glimpse of her defiant spirit was a small gift from above.

We celebrated the tiniest victories, watching her eat one single puff when her body was finally able. I took a video and sent it to every family member and friend in our circle. It felt as monumental as a college graduation.

It broke my heart each time she asked to go "that way" toward the elevator, which she adorably called "the alligator," because she knew it meant going home. Her small hands, her brave little voice, her constant longing for home; all of it gutted me.

By day six, she was home.

Home, of course, was still Cody's childhood bedroom, with our suitcases piled in corners and medication spreadsheets taped to the walls. Twenty doses a day, meticulously tracked with color-coded highlighters and alarms on our phones. Some days felt like running a marathon without ever leaving the kitchen counter.

Two weeks post-transplant, Addie was unstoppable. Parks, storytime, backyard chases with Mili—her body carried her forward with a strength I could hardly believe. Her liver numbers climbed steadily into healthy ranges. The plan for "cleanup chemo" loomed, but for now, we tried to savor every untouched moment.

We were sitting at the kitchen counter, Play-Doh everywhere, when our oncology doctor called with the pathology report. My hand shook as I answered.

The tumor margins were negative, meaning they got all the cancer in the area, and the tumor itself was 80 percent dead.

Relief was an ocean that washed over me in a single breath. The chemo had worked. We would press forward with the same cocktail that had carried us thus far. It would be grueling, but we had a path. A plan. A fighting chance.

To celebrate Easter, we held a backyard egg hunt. I watched Addie stumble through the tall grass, her tiny fingers clasping brightly colored eggs, her laughter lifting into the spring air. Every step, every smile, was a defiant act against everything cancer had tried to steal from us.

There were signs of battle, of course. The steroids made her mood swing wildly. Her eyelashes thinned to wisps. Strangers sometimes mistook her and Mili for twins, both with their soft bald heads and mischievous grins, but one look at Addie's full set of teeth gave away her hard-earned seniority.

Still, we pressed on. I took her to storytime at the library just nine days after her transplant because I needed to pretend, even just for an hour, that we were normal again. But normal did not come easily. Underneath the joyful noise of our new life was a deeper current. The letter we knew we wanted to write.

How do you express eternal gratitude and unbearable sorrow in the same words? What do you say to a family who lost their child while yours lived?

Weeks passed after the transplant before I could even bring myself to pick up a pen. I sat in front of blank pages, paralyzed.

Eventually, the words came, not for them, but for me.

The letter we sent through the Donor Alliance read:

> This letter is a first attempt at thanking you and expressing our very sincere condolences for your loss. We don't know you, or your precious loved one who has passed, yet our family has been made whole again through your shared sacrifice. The liver that she received through transplant has fostered such a grand new beginning, and the moment she awoke from surgery felt as joyous as the day she was born.
>
> We could never repay you for this opportunity for our daughter, but we hope that knowing what a positive difference it has made in our lives provides inspiration and solace in yours. It is our desire that you can cherish Addie's future with us, knowing that it is a direct result of the miraculous gift that we received from you. We truly admire your courage for giving our daughter the chance at a beautiful life.

We mailed it, and then waited.

We updated our address three times during Addie's year of treatment, always making sure the donor agency could find us, should the family ever choose to respond.

They never did.

Months passed without a response. I learned that was common. Families needed time, sometimes a lifetime, to process what had been given and what had been lost. Still, I carried the thought of them with me, quietly, in the background of every milestone Addie reached.

Nine years later, I am still waiting. Still hopeful that, one day, they will write back. Sometimes, I wonder if it is the response I long for, or simply the confirmation that they received our gratitude, that they know they made a difference.

I think about writing again, updating them on all the moments their gift made possible, even if our story took a turn no one could have predicted. I think about telling them that their child's legacy lives on in every memory, every smile, every breath we still carry forward.

But for now, I hold onto the purity of that first letter.

Addie's new life was just beginning.

And so was our journey of hope.

Dear Addie, thank you for ... blessing me with the opportunity to see life from another angle.

5

Chasing Hope

"Once you choose hope, anything's possible."

−Christopher Reeve

When your child's survival depends on toxins so strong you can't even touch them without protective gloves, hope becomes your oxygen. But chasing hope through chemotherapy was an exhausting and complicated dance; a two-step forward, one-step-back rhythm defined our days.

It was on Addie's fifth round of chemo when I realized just how toxic hope could feel. Sitting beside her in the audiology room, the air was heavy with anticipation. The audiologist's face said it all before her words did. Addie was losing her hearing from Cisplatin, the same drug that was meant to save her life. My heart sank. Hope felt confusingly cruel.

But even chemo couldn't fully steal our joy. At home, Addie still had her park days with family, giggling as she raced to the slide, legs pumping with just enough strength to climb, then flying down into Macca's waiting arms−my mom, who became "Macca" when Addie, still learning to speak, couldn't quite say Grandma. My mom owned that quirky name like her badge of honor. She would push Addie on the swings for as long as Addie wanted, and every time Addie yelled "higher!", Macca would laugh and push with all her might, as if the sky itself was something she could give her. She loved Addie fiercely, and she loved me, too, always trying to care for us both—even when I resisted.

My brother, Greg, flew in with his family whenever they could, crossing several time zones just to be there. They played with Addie when she had the energy, and sat beside us when she didn't. That meant everything. We were a small, tightly woven family—never perfect, but always present when it mattered most.

Clinic visits for magnesium, potassium, and fluids turned into a repetitive ordeal, an exhausting routine. Our lives became measured in blood counts, transfusions, and dreaded fevers. Every spike in temperature signaled another emergency room trip and another sleepless night.

I remember standing in line at the hospital's platelet donation center one day, desperate to give something back, to feel useful in this powerless battle. When they told me I couldn't donate because of a medication I was taking, my frustration was overwhelming. I felt I was failing Addie by not replenishing the very lifeline that she so frequently relied on.

After months of relentless treatments, we reached what we hoped would be our final round of chemo. The end was so close we could taste it. It was May, just before Mili would turn one, and she was finally able to play with Addie in her hospital crib because flu season had ended. For six-months, the girls were apart so much of the time because Mili was not allowed on the seventh floor to visit, and that crushed me to my core. When Mili was finally able to visit, their laughter echoed through the hospital halls like music, warming the coldest corners of my heart. I could see that they missed each other equally. Their joy transcended the room. Watching them together was pure magic, a brief glimpse of normalcy and a moment I deeply cherished during the relentless storm.

But as much as hope was within reach during that final round, Addie's numbers told another story. When her AFP level did not decrease as much as predicted for remission, but rose up slightly, the air in the oncology ward felt thicker, heavier. Our doctors didn't have answers, only more tests. Cody remained silent, but I could read the doubt on his face. He never voiced his fears, not clearly. But I knew they haunted him, especially in quiet moments when we were alone.

The day of Addie's chemo bell-ringing was supposed to mark victory, our triumph over cancer. It was the day every cancer family dreamed of, the milestone of survival, of life beyond chemo. Nurses gathered, smiles filled the hallway, and Cody and I stood nearby with uneasy hearts. Addie tugged the rope on the bell with innocent joy, unaware of the uncertainty we held deep inside.

After we arrived home that night, Cody and I had a discussion in private. Our words were filled with something between pride and anxiety. "It happened," Cody said softly, "but her AFP numbers are rising again ..."

"I know," I said. "I don't know what to do, but I don't think we are done with chemo."

We stopped ourselves, as if speaking our fears out loud would make them any less painful. But we already knew what we feared was true: This fight was far from over.

Dear Addie, thank you for ... showing me how precious the smallest moments are, even when we couldn't yet see the storm ahead.

Most people look forward to the beautiful weather during the end of May in Fairbanks. Cool, crisp sun-filled air with temperatures in the fifties gives way after the snow breakup, and the summer solstice is around the corner. There is over twenty hours of daylight, and the mosquitoes have not yet come out to play.

I boarded the plane in Denver, leaving my daughter's side for the first time since she was born, for a marathon forty-six hour trip to pack up and sell our house in Alaska. After the transplant, we knew the only option for us was to move, because the local hospital there just could not support her post-transplant treatment. Colorado was always the destination we were planning on after we retired from the military, so we decided to make that move a few years sooner.

When I arrived, everything was just as I left it before our vacation. A fresh pack of diapers was in the diaper caddy and clothes that no longer fit the girls were folded in the top drawer. As I was packing up the house, very little of what we owned seemed important enough to bring.

I whittled down our belongings to just personal items. I packed journals, clothes, and some kitchen items we had received as gifts from our wedding. I sold almost all our furniture. I even parted with most items from Addie's nursery, which were some of the hardest things to let go of. However, there was no question I wanted to keep my rowing machine. It was a crucial piece of workout equipment post-baby during the frigid winters when jogging outside was not an option. I felt personally attached to it. It may have cost more to move than buying a new one, but I was not in my right mind at the time.

While I was there for less than two days, Addie's former preschool teacher, Susan, put on a fun-run in the town of Fairbanks to raise money and honor Addie. I could not have asked for a more beautiful sight with kids working a lemonade stand, bouncy houses, a preschool art auction, and a petting zoo. That made my heart so happy during such a trying time for our family. I gave away most of her toys from our house during that event, and that felt special.

Only a few hours later, it was time to depart Alaska and all its precious memories. I wanted to see Addie so desperately. I missed her so much and could not wait to give her a giant hug.

The exhaustion hit me before I even boarded the plane to Colorado. I'd been awake for nearly fifty hours, packing up the house, cleaning every corner, packing up Addie's favorite toys, and desperately holding it all together. It was the kind of exhaustion that made you feel like you were floating just above your body, watching yourself stumble through each moment. The kind of exhaustion I had only ever felt during my mountain climbing days. The kind of exhaustion that settled deep into your bones and made you question your life choices.

The universe, or maybe the airline gods, had chosen that moment to give me a lesson in what "tired" really meant. Just before I left for the airport, one of my friends who saw me off, handed me a sleeping pill, Ambien. I knew I wasn't supposed to take medication prescribed for someone else, but it was a moment of desperation, and anything I had ever known went out the window. The only thing I knew was that Cody had taken it in the past as a fighter pilot. They took it when they needed to reset their sleep schedules on a deployment. Well, the trip felt like a deployment to me, so I felt entitled. I had a child with cancer and a house to move; I didn't have time to think about anything else, especially the details of taking an Ambien during my trip home. With a shrug, I accepted her offering and took it.

The first flight left at one in the morning and was only four hours long, but it felt as if I had passed through several lifetimes in the span of it. As soon as I sat down, I was out cold. My head drooped.

My body sank into the seat. I couldn't have cared less about the in-flight snacks or the dimmed lights or anything. I was gone.

But then, there was a tap on my shoulder. I opened one eye, and a flight attendant was smiling at me, perhaps thinking I was just another well-rested traveler. "Miss, you need to get off the plane. It's being cleaned."

Wait, what?

I blinked hard, trying to focus, but my brain throbbed under invisible pressure, refusing to cooperate. I stumbled off the plane in a daze. The airport looked desolate, just me and the occasional ghost of someone else who had been awake too long.

That's when the Ambien really kicked in. The room spun. My legs were jelly. My eyelids weighed about a ton. I made my way to the nearest women's bathroom and, with all the grace of a toddler in a snowstorm, I crawled into the corner of the stall and collapsed onto the cold tile floor.

I closed my eyes for what I thought was a few minutes. I think people asked me if I was OK, some concerned, others probably wondering if I was just camping for the night. "I'm fine," I mumbled, trying to sound like I had any grasp on reality. "I just need to rest."

Rest? Sure, let's call it that. I think I was passed out in a way that would've made anyone question the definition of "rest."

At some point, maybe an hour later, I dragged myself out of the bathroom stall, a zombie on a mission. I had to make my connecting flight. I had no idea what time it was. My body was still floating outside itself.

I found the first person I could, a security guard in a bright yellow vest. "I need to get to my next gate," I muttered, already regretting my life choices. I told him about the pill, the nap, and my current daze. He nodded with an understanding smile, as though I was just another wanderer caught in the airport abyss.

"You missed your connection," he said gently. "But don't worry, I'll take care of it."

And so, like a small, disoriented child, I climbed into a golf cart, was shuttled through the empty airport, and rebooked my flight. "I'll take you there," he promised, driving me as though I were a VIP through the deserted terminal.

I finally made it to my gate, still clueless about what time it was. My brain was a cloud of confusion, and all I wanted was to lie down somewhere soft. But there was no time. I had to get home. My daughter had her post-transplant scan today, and we were supposed to meet with the doctor. I couldn't be late. The man set an alarm on my phone, telling me it would go off when it was time to board. He seemed to know, deep down, that I was too foggy to do anything for myself.

I didn't know how much time passed before I picked up my bags from the carousel at my home airport, my brain still wading through molasses. And then, Cody called. I felt an odd, preemptive dread when I saw his name, a dread that sliced right through the remaining fog.

"We got the results," he said, his voice tight.

I'd missed the appointment. I braced myself, expecting to hear that her cancer marker had gone down, that she was getting better. I'd believed it so fiercely, every fiber of my being rooting for her. She had felt better these past few months after the liver transplant. She was smiling. She was playing. She was alive.

But then he spoke the words that stopped me cold.

"The cancer's relapsed and metastasized," he said, his voice thick. "It's in her lungs, and it's aggressive. Stage IV now."

Every movement of my body stopped, my heartbeat slow and distant.

But then, something else. A flicker. A surge of something.

No, no, no. This is just a setback. She is strong. She is a fighter. The cancer can't have the final word. I won't let it.

I didn't even ask what was next. I didn't need to. I knew what had to happen. We would fight it. Stronger chemotherapy, new treatments, new possibilities. I could feel my heart pounding, not in fear, but in a defiant hope.

She was going to beat this.

Reflecting back years after I missed this encounter with the doctor, I wonder how it would have changed my outlook if I was there. What would have been different if I had never taken the Ambien, and never missed my flight?

Cody later told me that the doctor had suggested we take her home and stop treatment that day. That he had said she had little chance of surviving or even making it till her third birthday. Maybe if I'd heard that from the doctor, it would have sunk in. But I didn't hear that. What I heard was that she was strong, and we could make it.

Years later, Cody admitted something he had kept from me at the time: He had already started pre-grieving at that moment. Maybe it was better that way. But I wasn't giving up on her–not ever. Miracles happened. I knew it, without a shred of doubt.

My mother believed in miracles too. The moment she heard the word "relapse," a quiet fire ignited beneath her ribs. Like me, she was not one to sit still in the face of fear. Addie was her grandchild, and I was her daughter; she was fighting for both of us.

My mom, a retired teacher with an insatiable hunger for understanding, dove headfirst into research, scouring forums, journals, and obscure medical corners of the internet that I would not have found if I had tried. She had witnessed cancer take its toll on members of our extended family, had seen what could go wrong when the right care was not administered, and she was determined not to let that happen again.

But she was not just searching for answers, she was looking for relief, for me. The same way I was looking for relief for Addie. My mom was a natural caregiver, deeply empathetic and fiercely loyal, and when I crumbled, she stood up straighter. She carried the torch of hope when mine flickered. And at that moment, we both needed her light.

I wrote this crushing passage to our family and friends when we found out about the relapse:

> The results of Addie's CT scan showed that the cancer has now spread to her lungs. We are in complete shock as we were expecting to get a clean bill of health for the cancer and move on with her transplant treatment.
>
> She has 24 nodules of cancer in her lungs, which is more than our doc (of 30 years on staff here) has ever seen. He has never seen a case like hers and we are now in the process of researching funded experimental studies in Colorado as well as around the entire country. He believes her cancer has built up a resistance to her chemo. The cells in her liver might have been "kept at bay" while she was going through the first

few rounds of chemo, however, after the transplant while on immunosuppression therapy they were able to thrive despite the post-transplant chemo.

Her cancer is now extremely aggressive, and time is of the essence.

We have very little emotional capacity to communicate right now, as we are entrenched in doctor meetings and caring for Addie. The path ahead causes grave concern, which is an understatement. There are no known successful treatments, so we will put even more faith in our care team and do as much world-wide research on our own. What little info we have found for treatment possibilities is further complicated due to the liver transplant. Obviously the cancer treatment takes priority, but our little fighter has a big struggle ahead.

Dear Addie, thank you for ... teaching me about the power of hope and miracles.

6

The Gift of Moments

"When we are no longer able to change a situation,
we are challenged to change ourselves."

—Viktor E. Frankl

It's amazing what you'll do when your child turns one. In my case, for Mili, it meant ignoring the exhaustion of hospital nights, my cramped fingers delicately tying layers of lavender, teal, and white tulle together, hoping the tutu looked as perfect as my Pinterest inspiration. It also meant spreading thick purple frosting onto Mili's flower shaped cake that I made from a mold my mother picked up at a garage sale. Joy felt foreign, but necessary, a lifeline in a sea of uncertainty.

As Mili laughed, stomping her little foot eagerly into the soft layers of cake, I couldn't help but smile. She was running around in the backyard grass when I set the cake down in front of her to capture the moment. Her delight was uncontainable, nothing like Addie's first birthday, where my mom and I had strategically placed Cheerios on top of the cake just to entice her to touch it for a photo. Mili, though, took no convincing. Her chubby toes squished into the frosting, giggling uncontrollably as I captured the chaos on camera. My heart swelled, but the familiar ache returned instantly, a bittersweet reminder of the girl who wasn't here. I felt guilty for smiling while Addie was trapped in a hospital bed, facing a fierce fight yet again.

In the quiet aftermath of cake-smashing bliss, my mind drifted to the day Mili was born. Like Addie's birth, it was memorable. It was preceded by two months of my parents living with us, because we were not sure if Mili would come early too. They watched as I ate bizarre foods to spark labor and walked endlessly in circles around our dirt-road neighborhood in the days before her due date. Those times were not my finest moments. I was grateful for their presence, but embarrassed by my impatient attitude. I was so done with being pregnant again!

Then, early one morning, the contractions started getting worse. We left Addie with my parents and headed to the hospital, making it just in time. I nearly collapsed in the parking lot. I was prepared to use my rusty hypnobirthing tactics once again, but this time it was different. I could not breathe deeply to relax, only maintain my heavy breathing while in excruciating pain. This labor seemed to be going much faster than Addie's.

I was rushed into an overly crowded delivery room full of fourteen interns who had no business witnessing what was about to unfold. My hypnobirthing was not working. The nurse repeated warnings about an infamous "ring of fire." I had never heard that term, but I could only imagine what she was describing. "I want the epidural now!" I shouted repeatedly, abandoning any notion of a drug-free delivery. *Forget bravery, just give me relief!* At that point, it was too late for medication; the pain nearly made me lose consciousness. And then she was here.

Savoring the time holding Mili in my arms, I marveled that childbirth could feel like surviving a natural disaster. It was the worst pain imaginable at the time, yet ironically, years later, it would pale in comparison to watching my child suffer cancer's cruel grip.

Now that memory seemed almost quaint as I wrestled with a far heavier burden. One year later, Addie's GI tract was ravaged, pneumatosis had inflamed her bowels, and anxiety and stomach cramps held her captive. Doctors filled her body with antibiotics and pain meds, leaving her stomach empty and her spirit desperate for comfort. No meals, no liquids. Watching her struggle, knowing her greatest joy in the hospital was food, broke my heart a little more each hour. Addie was in isolation, unable to visit the playroom, and the days blurred into an endless monotony.

Yet, I forced myself to embrace the fleeting happiness of Mili's messy cake escapade. I celebrated one daughter, even as my heart ached for the other. Because what I had learned was this: moments mattered. Whether joyful, devastating, or bittersweet—moments mattered. They shaped us, taught us, and reminded us that even within heartbreak, joy still existed.

Dear Addie, thank you for ... allowing me the time with Mili that she and I so desperately needed.

On one rare afternoon, we ventured off the seventh floor to the cafeteria for a bit of fresh air; well, as fresh as hospital air can be. We grabbed salads—we were trying to make healthy choices, even in the chaos. I remember looking down at the lettuce in my bowl, thinking it was a small, normal thing to hold on to. Addie, perched in her little red wagon, looked so content, so innocent.

But then she started vomiting. And with the vomit, there was blood and a nosebleed that wouldn't stop. We looked at each other in a mix of confusion and weariness, but this wasn't our first rodeo. *She's been through worse. This is just another bump in the road.*

We made our way back up to the seventh floor, trying to pretend like nothing was out of the ordinary. When we walked into the room, our nurse was waiting for us, and as soon as we told her what had happened, the change in her expression was instant. The calm, professional demeanor disappeared, replaced by something I couldn't quite read. The nurse barely hesitated before moving into action.

The nurse's finger slammed the button on the wall, the echo of it reverberating through the room. "Code blue," I heard over the loudspeaker. I had seen it happen in movies where the patient went into cardiac arrest and the team began CPR. I had read about it in textbooks. I knew this meant a life-threatening situation was unfolding. I was crippled with fear. This was my baby. The air in the room turned thick, heavy with a weight I didn't know how to bear. *Are we going to lose her right now? For good? I'm not prepared for this. This can't be happening.*

Addie's vitals were crashing. Various medical professionals began swarming around her in a surreal way. It felt like I was watching a scene from a medical drama, except this wasn't fiction. This was real. The room began to fill with voices, yet there was one sound that cut through it all, "This *is* a code blue."

Seconds later, the doors swung open, and in stormed the emergency team. They moved with calm purpose that didn't match the chaos inside my chest. The most striking figure among them was the young doctor.

He looked like he had walked straight off a Hollywood movie set. Seriously. I mean, was this real life? I could barely focus on anything else. He was tall, well-groomed, and far too attractive to be standing in a hospital room during a code blue. He looked so young, I wondered if he even went to medical school. *How is this beautiful young actor going to save my child?*

I couldn't help but think, *Is this a joke? Am I on some hidden camera show?* But, of course, this was real. My daughter was in grave danger, and this incredibly good-looking doctor wasn't just a pretty face, he was in charge, and he was working with a team that moved with precision. He spoke to us calmly, explaining everything as they worked, trying to keep us grounded. I had done basic EMT training years ago, but at that moment, I felt completely out of my depth.

I watched them hook up IVs, administer fluids. She needed blood and platelet transfusions. For about ten minutes, the room was a whirlwind of action. I wanted to look away, but I couldn't. I wanted to scream, but I was too afraid to make a sound. Then, almost as suddenly as it had started, the team began to slow down.

The doctor nodded at us and exchanged a few words with his team. "She's stable," he said, glancing at the monitor. Then he looked at us. "You brought her back up at the right time."

I stared at him, my throat too tight to speak. I could only nod, my hands still gripping the rail of her hospital crib to hold me up. "Is she going to be OK?" Cody asked, barely above a whisper.

"For now," he said.

Then, like they were finished filming, they turned around and left, off to save the next child in need. It was over. They had done what they came to do. Addie was stabilized.

I was left in a daze. The hardest part was realizing that it wasn't over. It wasn't a dramatic movie scene that would resolve itself in an hour. This was our life now. This was our reality.

The Hollywood doctor, unreal as he seemed, had done his job. He had saved her life. My emotions were a jumble of relief, exhaustion, and disbelief. There were no credits rolling, no dramatic music, and no happy ending. But we were alive, and Addie was too.

It was only hours later, after everything had calmed down, that I fully realized what had just happened. My hands trembled as I looked at her, pale but still breathing, still with us. *We almost lost her.*

But she was here. And as the hours stretched on, I held on to that relief with everything I had.

Dear Addie, thank you for ... the distraction of a Hollywood doctor during one of my most trying moments.

The sign in the lobby boasted, "Best Children's Hospital for Cancer, *U.S. News & World Report.*" But relapse is an unknown territory with cancer, no matter where you are.

At the hospital parents' group the week prior, we met a mother whose teenage son had faced his cancer reoccurring four times over twelve years. Her story hit me with colossal force. It was daunting to imagine living our life of uncertainty for another decade. As I listened to her story, my grip tightened around the hope I desperately needed to protect. I refused to believe that her reality could ever become ours.

St. Jude's had reported two cases in history when Hepatoblastoma patients displayed metastasis to the brain. Addie's doctors were concerned, but we exhaled with a sigh of relief when her brain scan came back negative that day.

That's the harsh truth about cancer: Answers rarely come neatly packaged. Just when you think you understand, reality shifts beneath you, leaving you searching for solid ground.

We'll always wonder what would have turned up on her scans if we had received the liver transplant call just one day later. Would we have seen the metastasis in her lungs then? If it had been found, she would have been removed from the transplant list. Or did it really just spread so aggressively *after* the transplant, when she was immunosuppressed? We'll never know.

One evening at home after one of Addie's relapse treatments, I received a voicemail while in the shower—the results of her latest AFP test was in. This test always kept us on pins and needles because we could usually speculate what the cancer was doing based on the reported level. It was a major factor when making treatment decisions. If numbers went down, it meant the drugs were killing the cancer. But if the number went up, the chemo wasn't working and her disease was progressing. The number would generally double every five days, because that is the known half-life of this protein. This meant a change in therapy was necessary.

"I just called to report her test results of 480,000," the nurse, unfamiliar with AFP testing, said casually in a message.

The nurse's voice echoed through my mind, each digit landing harder than the last. My body stiffened, breath catching sharply in my chest.

What do you mean, 480,000? I thought internally as I listened.

How could Addie's AFP level jump from 23,000 to almost half a million in a single week? We had somewhat expected the number to double as a familiar trend of ineffective chemo, but nothing like this. *It's not possible.* Her brain scan was clear, yet there it was, a cold, harsh reality left casually on voicemail. Just another day for the nurse, but a gut-wrenching twist of fate for us.

Has the cancer taken over her entire body in just one week? Is this the end? I questioned everything, her treatment, our choices, even my own instincts.

I frantically responded by calling back, only able to leave words of concern for our medical team. I spent the night pacing our bedroom, a bitter storm of dread and helplessness churning inside me. Addie lay quietly in our bed, her face pale from the treatment, oblivious to the devastating news I'd just heard. For hours, I searched medical journals, message boards, and anything that would offer me an explanation—hope or despair, I just needed answers.

I had learned early on that "practicing medicine" was exactly that: practice. Doctors and nurses didn't always know the answers. How could they? My daughter was one patient among hundreds, and no one would fight for her like I would. But as I searched my brain for answers, for options, the thought haunted me, *What if there really is nothing left to do?*

Sleep was out of the question that night, and when dawn finally broke, my eyes were dry and burning, my head pounding. The phone rang at 8:04 a.m. It was the nurse returning my desperate call. Her voice was hesitant and unassuming.

"Her AFP is at 48,000, not 480,000. I'm so sorry. It was my mistake."

The relief was immense, yet brief. Anger and frustration quickly filled the gap. Human error was understandable, but when it was your child's life, decimal points mattered. I forgave her days later, but the harsh lesson lingered: double-check everything. Always.

Dear Addie, thank you for … teaching me how important it is to question everything. I promise to never stop searching for answers, for you.

One afternoon, after an exhausting call with our insurance company, our hospital social worker approached quietly. She must have heard my raw and endless battle against the robotic person on the other end of the line. I had been trying to get a new medication covered for Addie. She discreetly passed a $50 gift card onto the hospital tray. It wasn't a large sum of money, but enough to cover my copay so I could use the pharmacy in the hospital.

The relief it provided was priceless.

That card meant no fighting with insurance that day. It meant I didn't have to drive across town to get a new medication to save a few dollars at a participating pharmacy. I could simply walk downstairs, collect Addie's meds, and know that one small piece of my struggle was taken care of. It was more than a card; it was peace, compassion, understanding, and dignity all wrapped in one tiny gesture.

Dear Addie, thank you for ... helping me see that kindness can appear when you least expect it–and exactly when you need it most.

Timing is everything, and sometimes timing is a bitch.

Addie was hooked up to her eighth round of chemo just two hours before we got word that her AFP number had doubled. Had we known just two hours earlier, we would have changed course. My heart broke knowing she was enduring the harshest chemicals, knowing they likely wouldn't help. Watching her immune system crumble, the endless blood draws, constant infusions, and infections–it all felt cruel and futile. And yet, it was the only option we'd had.

When the doctor explained that many cancers, like Addie's, could become resistant to chemo, it crushed me in a way I had never imagined possible. "We'll try another round and see," they would say, but each cycle took a little piece of Addie and me away. Trial and error felt barbaric.

As we contemplated lung surgery, the prospect was overwhelming. Each decision carried heavy implications, either further damaging Addie's small body with surgery or risking chemotherapy that might no longer work. The choice felt impossible, the responsibility immense. Every doctor's visit was filled with endless waiting, anxiety coiling tighter with each passing minute.

The reality of Addie's suffering was heartbreaking, but we clung to fleeting moments of joy, tiny glimpses of normalcy. Her smiles, though rare now, were more precious than ever. Her laughter became our medicine, reminding us to treasure each moment.

I wrote to family and friends:

> I so desperately want to see a direct correlation between how crappy Addie feels and how much the chemo is working, but that is just not how it works. The chemo is destroying her immune system and GI tract, though it may be doing absolutely nothing to the cancer.
>
> In fact, it may even be allowing the cancer to thrive, which makes me extremely infuriated. The bottom line is the trial and error part of finding the right chemo just sucks on all accounts, especially since a few months ago post liver transplant we thought we were going to walk away cancer free. I think we are still in disbelief due to the rarity of her case, but Addie's steadfast strength keeps us all going.

Chemo treatment was a marathon of endurance and pain. Days blended into nights; sleep was a precious commodity. Addie spent weeks screaming that her tummy hurt, every fifteen minutes, day and night. Her small hands pressed mine onto her stomach, pleading, "Please rub my tummy, Mommy."

I rubbed until my shoulders burned, repeating quietly under my breath, "Wax on, wax off," just like Mr. Miyagi in the *Karate Kid* movie I saw when I was twelve-years-old. Each stroke became a mantra, a desperate attempt to distract us both from reality.

My morning runs became a saving grace. The rhythmic pounding of my shoes on the pavement, the crisp Colorado air burning my lungs, all of it provided a small measure of sanity. In the Air Force, physical fitness wasn't just encouraged, it was required. I had spent decades conditioning my mind and body to endure challenges, pushing through barriers of pain and exhaustion to prove something to myself, to the world. But cancer didn't care about my military training, the mountains I had climbed, or the pain I had already endured. It challenged every mental and physical boundary I ever had.

Dear Addie, thank you for ... teaching me that sometimes strength is quiet, persistent, and deeply personal.

Our family has been knee deep in medical journal research—as well as diarrhea. Just when we thought we had figured out how to survive the rollercoaster of chemotherapy, timing treatments, managing fevers, calculating dosages like amateur pharmacists, we hit a wall. A smelly, unpredictable, utterly exhausting wall.

We changed thirty-five diapers that day.

Cody, in one of his moments of comic genius during our most sleep-deprived week, issued what he called a military warning order to our friends and family. It read like an official report, and honestly, it might as well have been.

> **BLUF (Bottom Line Up Front):** Christina and Cody have been unsuccessful with **OPERATION CONTAINMENT.**
>
> **MISSION OBJECTIVE:** Retain diarrhea material within close perimeter of Addie's body.
>
> **HISTORICAL CONTEXT:** Recent events in civilian locales have left trails of tears and poop on the floor of movie theaters and REI, causing significant discomfort to the principal.
>
> **COURSES OF ACTION:**
>
> 1. No public events—Pros: cheap. Cons: no fun.

2. Layered diaper approach—Pros: stocks will rise for Huggies and Pampers. Cons: expensive until Wall Street reacts.

3. Garbage bag pants—Pros: cheap, trendy, disposable. Cons: Addie may continue this fashion statement later in life.

He read it aloud with a completely straight face while I sat hunched over a spreadsheet tracking bowel movements and magnesium levels, desperate to keep her electrolytes stable enough to avoid another hospital stay. It was ridiculous. It was absurd. And I laughed so hard, I cried.

That night, we changed six more diapers in the dark while whispering strategy as though we were covert operatives on a mission. Because even through the chaos of pediatric oncology, there were moments when we had to choose humor, otherwise, we would lose ourselves. Cody was extremely good at it, especially when I wasn't.

The call came at 4:57 p.m. I was sitting on a swivel chair at Ashlie's kitchen island, trying unsuccessfully to remain still. The comforting scent of taco meat filled the air as Addie and Ashlie's son, Everest, laughed, popping their heads out of a cardboard box, delighting in each surprise appearance.

When the phone rang, my heart skipped a beat. It was the renowned doctor I had desperately reached out to about clinical trials for Addie's relapse. A doctor my mom had found. Eagerly, I asked him about the trial treatments mentioned in my email, and his voice held cautious acknowledgment.

Then came his question that shattered my hope instantly: "Have you considered taking her to Disneyland?"

I fell to the floor, overwhelmed. At that moment, hope vanished. I'm not sure that conversation got any easier for doctors no matter how many times they executed it. Addie's oncologist had gently danced around the subject, and others had hinted that she had no plausible options left, but I hadn't truly heard it until that word, "Disneyland," reached my ears. It was a suggestion to make her happy, to give her joy rather than struggle through more treatment–since the treatment would likely not work.

I was desperately seeking a clinical trial, anything that could save my daughter. But after that call, a dark reality began to take hold, and a new kind of despair settled within me.

He was telling me to give up, but how could we accept the unimaginable?

That evening, with all the confusion and emotional turmoil, I began to plan lifelong memories.

Dear Addie, thank you for ... reminding me that cardboard boxes can be a child's biggest delight. You made me smile even when my heart was crushed.

7

Life with the Windows Down

"When a great adventure is offered, you don't refuse it."

—Amelia Earhart

Has one word ever changed your entire world? For me I thought it was "cancer." That day at Ashlie's, it was "Disneyland." But this would feel worse.

Sitting alone in the sterile quiet of the doctor's office, I felt trapped. My eyes burned as tears raced uncontrollably down my cheeks, dripping onto the floor. There was nowhere to hide, no way to escape. The doctor's careful, compassionate eyes watched as he gently repeated the word I had been refusing to acknowledge: hospice. Until that moment, I had convinced myself they meant palliative care: comfort, support, and perhaps temporary. But now, reality flooded through me, stark and merciless.

I felt numb, paralyzed by a dread so intense it seemed to swallow me whole. This wasn't about temporary comfort; this was about facing an unbearable truth.

When I met with the hospice social worker, she saw my internal fear and the raw uncertainty etched across my face. "Our greatest joy," she said softly, "is seeing children graduate from hospice."

That simple sentence changed everything. In the darkest hour, she had given me back something I thought I had lost: hope. For me, hospice wasn't going to be about giving up. It was about choosing comfort, but also believing in miracles. I needed to see possibility even through profound uncertainty.

When everything else felt out of control, family was the only thing I could hold onto.

I called Greg the day we were told Addie would be placed in hospice. I could barely get the words out, and he didn't say much at first. There was a long pause, long enough for me to imagine him gripping the phone with both hands, staring at the floor, trying to steady his breath.

"I just received my orders. We have to move to Korea," he said. I was crushed. I knew he wanted to stay, to be close, to shoulder this with us. As an A-10 pilot, he did everything in his power to remain state-side, but we both knew what we gave up when we joined the Air Force. You don't always get to choose what's next. I could hear the heartbreak in his voice, though he tried to hide it behind the same quiet strength that had carried our family for years. He was granted a few extra months before he had to go, and we made the most of them. We built memories like they were sandcastles we knew the tide would soon reach. He and his family held Addie like every moment mattered, because it did. None of it was fair. But we were together now, and that part, that part we didn't waste.

Dear Addie, thank you for ... teaching me that hope can endure even in our most despairing moments, that somehow, you just know there is a way.

It started with a triple.

Not just any triple, Ichiro Suzuki's 3,000th career hit. Cody was ecstatic, soaking in the baseball glory, while Addie sat content in her Rockies stadium seat, dipping pretzel bites into fake cheese like it was gourmet. Then, moments later she had Dippin' Dots clutched in one hand and a lollipop in the other. More sugar than any child should have, but we didn't care. For her, the baseball game was about the food experience, and for one perfect afternoon, everything felt normal. Or at least, our version of normal.

Later that evening, still filled with stadium joy, we sat on the couch and turned on a documentary. It claimed cannabis could kill cancer. Not just ease the suffering, not just numb the nausea or calm the nerve pain, but actually destroy tumors. That was the moment it happened. That spark. The one you get when you have no real answers, no certainty, no finish line in sight, but something whispers, *What if this is the thing?*

I believed in that whisper. Desperately.

It was irrational; of course it was. But I had already traded in reason for hope a long time ago. If there was even the faintest possibility that we could make a cannabis concoction–some magical, barely legal blend of oil and strain–that might shrink Addie's tumors, I was in. We were both in. We had to be.

The process of finding someone who knew anything about cannabis dosing for children with cancer was a nightmare. There were vague recommendations, most of them aimed at seizure patients, but nothing that fit our reality. We were flying blind. And still, we moved forward.

The first dose made her giggly. She got ... high. There was no other way to say it. Addie was floaty and free, her eyes brighter than they had been in weeks. Cody and I sat in stunned silence, watching her happiness pour out like sunlight. We laughed, because what else do you do when your three-year-old is giggling from cannabis and you are secretly hoping it is killing her cancer? You laugh and pretend it makes perfect sense.

We adjusted the dosage quickly. It was never about the high. We wanted her to be comfortable. We wanted her pain-free. But secretly, quietly, I was waiting for the miracle. The story where the cancer just disappeared. Cured by something no one understood. The miracle that lived in the margins of every medical journal that said, "*Not* enough evidence yet."

And then, somehow, we made it. Forty-one weeks into treatment. Ten rounds of chemo. It felt like a surreal milestone. Not a finish line. More like a checkpoint in a race we never agreed to run. Addie's hair had come and gone and come again in patches. Her skin was pale, but glowing. Her smile still lit up the world.

She was off chemo now. She was feeling better than she had in months. We were riding that impossible wave where everything felt lighter, and we dared to hope. Maybe chemo was the problem. Maybe her body would fight now. Maybe it was strong enough on its own. Maybe, just maybe, her body would kill the cancer itself. Do the work for us. That was the madness of hope. It made sense in its own twisted way.

Her laugh had returned after ten rounds of chemo. Her appetite, too. She ate pizza and loaded her own sundaes with whipped cream and gummy worms. She danced around at story time in the library and jumped on the trampoline at the new indoor play gym. Her cheeks were flushed again. It was everything we wanted.

But then again, I saw her pause now and then while playing, her chest rising quickly, then settling again. Was she just out of shape from so much time in bed? Or was it beginning to hurt to breathe?

My answer came when the scan came back.

More nodules in her lungs. The cancer was growing. The MRI showed no spread to her brain, but I did not need a medical degree to know what this meant.

Our doctors proposed a Phase II study. A targeted therapy with a short list of success stories. We wanted to believe. We signed the papers, did the bloodwork, and scheduled everything. Then the company delayed the drug shipment. No medication. Just a vague reassurance that it might show up soon.

We were standing in the middle of a crossroad: new treatment or a trip to Disneyland.

And we chose Disneyland.

Not because we had given up. Not because we had lost faith in science or medicine or the microscopic magic of a molecule that might stop blood flow to a tumor. We chose Disney because Addie was smiling. She was feeling well. She wanted to run and jump and eat too much cotton candy and meet all the Disney princesses. We could not waste that, not on more waiting.

I had already fought the insurance company until my throat burned, trying to get Addie's tumor genetically tested. I did not care anymore about the red tape. Let her sample help someone else's child, if not mine. We were done playing by the rules.

So, we packed up her PEZ candy dispensers, her favorite movies on her iPad, and her Sadie, and went to the happiest place on earth. We left the study behind, for now.

There was still pain. There was still fear. But in that moment, we chose joy.

We boarded that plane with a suitcase full of supplements, an expired promise of medication, and a girl who still believed in magic. She smiled as we took off. Cody held her hand. I held the sliver of hope tucked in my chest. This tiny irrational belief that maybe, just maybe, there were miracles hiding in mouse ears and fairy dust.

Next stop: Disneyland.

Dear Addie, thank you for ... reminding us that joy does not wait for certainty.

I did not want to book the trip. Even now, that truth feels heavy to admit, but there it is. Like so many things in that season of life, it came wrapped in layers of guilt and guarded hope. Disneyland was the place you went when everything was OK, when your child was well and healthy and squealing about chips and cotton candy. It was not where you went when you were silently wondering whether your daughter would see her third birthday.

When my mom first brought up Make-A-Wish, I felt offended ... insulted even. I believed that organization was for families who could not afford a trip like that, or worse, for the ones who had already accepted the ending. I was not there yet. Not even close. In my mind, if I signed up for a "wish," I was somehow signing off on the possibility of her not making it. Like that trip would seal the fate I refused to acknowledge.

But somehow, under all that pride and defiance, I said yes. And maybe I did it hoping to prove the universe wrong. If this was the trip that people took when their child was dying, maybe we could reverse the narrative. Maybe we would go, laugh, eat overpriced snacks, and come back with Addie healthier than before. A twisted way to prove we were not done writing her story.

We could not have planned it ourselves. Make-A-Wish did everything. They thought of every detail, from car seats in the limo to a line pass that let us skip every wait. They even booked an airplane seat for Mili so we could fly in comfort without her on our lap. For the first time in months, we felt like a family traveling, not a family chasing down cancer appointments.

The morning the limo pulled into our alley, honking as though it had just arrived for a royal ball, the magic began. The girls sprinted to the balcony in matching Dory t-shirts, their joy spilling over the railing. Addie's face held pure wonder. I will never forget the look. It was the kind of glow you cannot fake. I half expected a team of animated birds to come out and help us pack.

Inside the limo, balloons floated cheerfully, Mickey grinned from the television screen, and there was an unreasonable amount of Doritos. It was chaotic and perfect. We tossed our bags, strapped in, and pulled away. I could hear "Let It Go" playing in my head, a soundtrack we didn't know we needed.

The hotel was modest, but charming, just a short walk from the gates of Disney. Our extended family had already arrived. Greg and his wife, Cristy, had mapped out the park like professionals; this was not their first rodeo. They were ready to squeeze every second of magic from this trip, especially since it might be some of the last moments they would get to spend with Addie before their move to Korea.

That night, the cousins jumped on the beds together, playing their made-up game they called "bootie bounce." I took a video, mostly because I knew it might be the only thing that got me through later. Addie's smile was so bright.

Disneyland hit differently when you were there to escape reality. Addie's face lit up the second she saw the giant Halloween pumpkins towering over the entrance. Halloween was her favorite: candy, costumes, the silliness of it all. Her eyes caught the castle immediately. "It's like the *Frozen* one," she gasped, and suddenly we were not in Anaheim anymore. We were in her world.

Every moment mattered. Her window of feeling good was narrow, so we moved quickly, but gently. We met Elsa and Anna, and she tucked herself shyly into Olaf's fuzzy arms. She soared above the park on an airplane ride, took a nap like a seasoned stroller tourist, and explored every gift shop like it was her job.

And then, the parade.

Addie sat on the curb with a tub of cotton candy almost the size of her torso. Blue and pink sugar stained her lips, and her eyes never left the street. The floats rolled past like a dream: Nemo, Buzz Lightyear, Ariel, and of course, Mickey and Minnie. Music played, dancers twirled, and Addie danced with them, her tiny arms waving, face glowing with the kind of joy that made you believe in magic.

We spent the next few days chasing laughter. From Cars Land in Disney Adventure, to the Minions at Universal, she knew every character from our endless hospital room movie marathons. She got winded sometimes. Her body was still recovering, still unsure how to catch up to her spirit. But I tried not to focus on that. I was learning to stay in the present.

Evenings were simple. We had a takeout picnic on the hotel floor, Addie curled up on my lap, exhausted from the fun. The cousins played bootie bounce, high on sugar and adrenaline, while I just watched. I watched so hard. I wanted to remember every detail: the way her cheeks dimpled when she laughed, the way her sister ran toward the noise, the way my family made space for joy, even when none of us knew what came next.

On the last day, we went to the Santa Monica Pier. Addie dipped her feet in the ocean with Cody by her side. The moment was still. We had been to mountains, glaciers, and eleven states … but she had never been to the beach. The salty air hit me in a way that almost knocked the breath from my lungs. I wanted to cry but not because I was sad. It was gratitude. It was the unbelievable truth that this moment was real.

The kids played in the sand. Addie collected shells with sandy fingers and ate more candy than I thought her chemo stomach could handle. On the pier, from her perch on the Ferris wheel, she giggled, watching her mom and her aunt Cristy defeat their husbands in carnival games. That part still makes me laugh.

I still flip through the photos and watch the videos. In them, Addie looks like happiness itself. And maybe she is. Maybe we all are.

That trip gave us something we never expected: presence. We stopped running from fear and fell, for a few days, into magic, into belief. Belief, not in perfect endings, but in perfect moments.

Dear Addie, thank you for … letting me see what I almost missed.

There are moments in life when the ordinary becomes sacred. Teaching your two-year-old to drive a car down a dirt road is not supposed to be one of them, but for us, it was.

It was crisp in the Colorado mountains, the kind of autumn weather that steals your breath before the altitude does. The leaves were unapologetically beautiful–blazing oranges, stubborn reds, soft yellows barely clinging to their branches. We stayed in a small wooden cabin at the YMCA camp in Granby, and Cody's parents joined us. I remember thinking how strange it was that the world could still look this beautiful while ours was falling apart.

That morning, Addie asked to drive.

And because we were no longer saying no to much of anything, Cody scooped her onto his lap with a theatrical, "Let's do it!"

She sat tall, as if her car seat days were long behind her. Cody's dad smiled at her from the passenger seat. Her little hands reached up and gripped the steering wheel with the fierce confidence of someone who believed they could fly if they just tried hard enough. Her face radiated pure joy.

There was no panic. No fear. No sense of the weight Cody and I carried in our hearts every day. There was just a little girl learning to steer down a winding dirt road with a delighted squeal and eyes wide enough to hold the sky.

It was the first and only time I would see her drive a car. I let myself feel the beauty and the pain, tangled together in a single breath I never wanted to release.

When we checked out of the camp, they told us not to pay. I insisted. They refused. Word had spread. It was the kind of generosity you never forget–quiet, graceful, and more meaningful than it looked on the surface. I tucked that moment into my heart.

After that, we boarded a flight for New York. Long Island was my childhood home, but this trip was for Addie. It felt urgent. Necessary. Maybe even final.

We had one mission for this trip: PEZ.

Addie was completely, irrationally, hilariously obsessed with those tiny chalky candies. I never understood why, but I also never questioned it. If PEZ was what brought her joy, then PEZ it would be.

The PEZ Visitor Center in Orange, Connecticut looked like Willy Wonka had consulted with a seven-year-old interior designer and said, "Go wild." As we pulled up, the massive PEZ dispenser sculpture loomed, a towering monument to childhood. Addie's whole face lit up.

Inside, a rainbow of dispensers stretched across decades of cartoon history: Mickey, Hello Kitty, Yoda, Garfield. She darted from case to case, wide-eyed; her tiny fingers pressed to glass, naming the characters in her own made-up accent. We were handed special VIP badges when we arrived and Addie proudly wore hers.

Built into the tile floor was an exhibit, a swirling galaxy of PEZ dispensers lit with electric neon colors like a sugary stained-glass window. Addie stared down, completely still, just absorbing it. I can still access this moment, still fresh in my mind.

Her awe was complete. Her joy, unfiltered. I had not seen her that captivated by something in weeks. I crouched next to her, trying not to blink, trying to memorize the curve of her smile, the way her fingers traced invisible lines over the glass, the whisper she gave the Minion dispenser: "You're my favorite."

That was why we came. We made it home with a suitcase full of PEZ and a heart full of memories we were not ready to label as lasts.

Hospice was going well, which is a strange sentence to write. Our nurse visited regularly. Our music and art therapists made the days feel lighter than they should have been. Cody flew back to Alaska briefly to finish selling the house, and I packed the girls up for a Thanksgiving celebration at a friend's house. It was a pre-holiday holiday, because two Thanksgivings felt like a reasonable request when time was no longer a guarantee.

Maintenance chemo had held things at bay, or so we believed. But the thing about this cancer was you never knew. We were completely blind between scans. Blind as a bat, and yet somehow clinging to the feeling that maybe, just maybe, if we loved her hard enough, we could keep her here.

Some days she looked well. Other days, I watched her sleep and counted every breath.

I foolishly held onto the idea that some unknown treatment would appear out of nowhere. That clinical trial we were not eligible for. That drug that was still waiting for FDA approval. That article someone's friend of a friend sent. I read them all. I memorized names of medications that sounded similar to magic spells. I pretended we had time.

I was terrified that we did not.

And yet, there was peace in the not knowing. We were no longer in and out of hospitals every other day. We stopped checking labs. We stopped measuring. We just started living. It was fragile. It was desperate. It was beautiful.

Being blind, sometimes, is bliss.

Addie's third birthday was just around the corner, and we were planning it with the kind of fervor most people save for weddings.

A little girl turning three should never feel like a monumental achievement, but for us, it did.

Dear Addie, thank you for ... reminding us that, even blind, we could still find happiness.

I do not know why I needed her to turn three. Maybe it gave me something to hold onto; a number, a moment, a finish line. Proof that we had made it further than expected after her relapse. Proof that she was still here, defying the odds. Or maybe I just wanted to say she died at three. As if that somehow sounded like we'd had more time. As if I could barter with time itself by simply naming it.

Addie's third birthday was more than a celebration. It was a dare to the universe. A full-hearted, tear-filled declaration that we were still here, still loving, still living, despite the clock ticking louder every day. Despite the dark cloud of a Stage IV diagnosis that hovered close behind our laughter, trying to swallow it whole. Her cancer had aggressively metastasized with no surgical removal options in sight.

Great Play, a mini jungle gym designed for toddlers, had always been Addie's sanctuary. I can still see her there: the way her tiny fingers gripped the slightly-raised balance ladder like it was the edge of a mountain, how her smile stretched across her whole face when she swung from the high swing, her little body flying through the air under a two-story ceiling, as though she had no cancer cells multiplying in her lungs. No transplant scar across her belly. No looming end. Just joy.

The owner of Great Play had never once charged us for a membership. He told us to bring her any time she felt well. No paperwork, no pressure, just open arms and a brightly painted room full of light and movement and freedom. I will never forget that kindness. In a world of sterile hospital beds and sharp needles, that place was both her sanctuary and mine.

So I decided: this was where we would celebrate. I invited our closest friends and family, the ones who had carried us through a year of unimaginable chaos. I wanted them to see Addie's face light up the way I did, to feel her joy reverberate through the room.

She wore a black and white polka dotted Minnie Mouse hat topped with a giant pink bow that somehow made her bald head invisible to me. All I could see was her radiance. It pulsed through her cheeks, through her bright eyes, through her every giggle as she twirled in the play gym.

Mary came, another mother I had met on the pediatric oncology floor. Her son, Isaac, was almost the same age as Addie. He was also bald, but his prognosis was brighter. Leukemia, they said, with promising treatments and solid remission odds. I could feel her hesitation stepping into our party, probably unsure if her presence would bring hope or grief. But our kids had bonded over hospital playrooms and a shared love for candy. We had bonded over the unspoken truth that only a cancer mom can fully grasp. Parallel paths that were now beginning to split. I did not know what that meant for our friendship, but that day, it did not matter. We were both just mothers watching our children be children, if only for an afternoon.

The cake was *Frozen* themed, of course. Jomama had gone all out. I still remember the candied ice crystals on top and the way Addie's eyes widened when she saw them. When we sang "Happy

Birthday," her little face glowed so brightly that I felt a pang of disbelief. How could a child so full of light be carrying something so dark inside her?

For a moment, I forgot. For a moment, she looked healed.

All the kids ran wild. The air was filled with laughter, echoes of squeaky shoes and cheerful screams. Parents chatted over plastic cups of juice, and there was so much life in that room I thought my heart might burst. I watched Addie swing, her arms spread wide. I was seeing the child she was always meant to be. The one without cancer. The one who might have danced on stage in a tutu or scraped her knees riding a bike down the sidewalk.

But I noticed something by the end of the party. A shift. Her body began to slow. Her eyes seemed a little distant, her spirit was already pulling slightly inward. The light was still there, but it flickered.

I kept the party going. What else could I do? I laughed too loudly. I cleaned up spilled juice and hugged guests as if I could physically hold onto time. Addie was still smiling, so we celebrated. We celebrated like she had a lifetime ahead.

I did not know what the future held. I still do not. But I had this moment. This party. This photo of Addie, eyes closed, soaring through the air like she knew she belonged to the sky.

That night, when I kissed her goodnight, she whispered, "I had a really fun day, Mommy."

And just like that, the world stood still. That small sentence held more than joy; it held presence, it held peace. I tucked it deep into my soul, right next to the sound of her laughter and the swing ropes creaking overhead. Those were the moments that kept me grounded when everything else felt unsteady.

I wrote in my journal. I wrote through my tears and my fear and my exhaustion.

It has been a year since Addie's diagnosis. She is now three. Chemo-resistant. No more proven treatments. But tonight ... she laughed.

And that was all I needed.

We were moving into our new house the following week. It had a deck that overlooked open space, and I already had plans to hang two swings, one for Addie and one for Mili. I pictured them there, side by side, the wind carrying their laughter out into the unknown. Maybe we would get that. Maybe we would not. But the image quietly lived inside me, a hidden wish waiting to come true.

While I clung to countless wishes, I also did everything I could to coax joy from Addie. As we prepared to move, I bought more Chinese takeout than any normal person should, just to keep Addie happy. She became obsessed with those crisp little cookies and the tiny slips of paper tucked inside. Eventually, I gave in and bought an entire tub of them. I laughed to myself when I did it. It was ridiculous. But also not at all ridiculous. Those were the things I could still control.

I did not know what would come next. I only knew that we were still standing. Still loving. Still hoping.

And at least for now, still celebrating.

Dear Addie, thank you for ... a wonderful memory from your third birthday that I will always cherish.

8

It's OK to Not Be OK

"Except for love, nothing you see will remain forever."

—Rumi

While on hospice, we still had adventures, but Addie was starting to slow down. One day she started mumbling confusing words. Cody was at work, and my mom and I were moving a few items into the new house. We headed to the hospital and told them we would be early for her appointment that day. I kept talking to Addie in the car, and when her voice faded away, my heart started racing so fast I thought it would burst. My foot slammed the gas.

By the time we made it to the hospital, she was unresponsive and felt lifeless when I picked her up out of the car seat. I parked in the parking garage as we would for a regular appointment, and ran in, panting, to the security desk with her in my arms, asking how to get to the emergency room from that entrance.

Is this the end? Is this how she will die? My heart stopped. I was not prepared.

I remember he paused to call someone on his walkie talkie because he could not tell me immediately. *How does the security person not know where the ER is?* I was furious, and then I looked up and saw the red sign above the hallway leading to the emergency department. I ran so fast, holding her tightly, thinking, *It's not time yet baby. It's not time.*

The doctors sprung into action and went to work, with me watching from the side lines like a bad episode of a medical drama—maybe the same one I mentioned earlier, but this time, there was no Hollywood doctor to distract me. They pumped her with meds and told me they thought she may have had a seizure. Just then, she started moving and I could hear her breathing loudly enough I knew this was not the final moment.

Hours later, when Cody arrived, they wheeled her back in after a brain MRI and told us the cancer had spread from her lungs to her brain. That was why she had a seizure, something I was not prepared for or aware could happen. Since the cancer was in her lungs, I was prepared for her to start having diminished breathing and possibly need oxygen supplementation, not an unresponsive and sudden seizure.

We emotionally adjusted and stayed a few nights in the hospital with electrodes on her head. We monitored seizures, listened to options for radiation, and learned all about seizure medication. But ultimately we had decided it was enough. We stopped trying to kill the cancer and wanted to focus on her comfort. We left that day with no plan to return.

I had been thinking about that day for a while now. I could not wrap my brain or my heart around what it would be like. How would I know when it was time to stop, and would Addie be able to tell me? This feeling was excruciating. I still don't know how I knew it was time, but I did. And Cody agreed. I just felt it in my heart. I needed to see Addie laugh and smile again.

Dear Addie, thank you for ... letting me know when it was OK to let go of treating the cancer and live each day that we had left to the fullest.

We had not even unpacked the kitchen boxes yet when my dad drilled the last swing into place beneath the deck. The air was brisk and crisp, the kind that carried hints of December in its breath. Addie was bundled in her red fleece jacket and her Minnie Mouse hat, her cheeks flushed from the cold. For that brief, magical hour, she was simply a child again, feet swinging, laughter echoing off the new siding of our just-moved-into home. "Higher, Macca!" she called out, and my mom obliged. Mili smiled on the swing next to her.

We opened presents every day. Not wrapped in paper with bows, but wrapped in urgency. I did not know how many more mornings we would have, so we treated each one like Christmas morning. The grandparents came, and we celebrated each moment as a gift. It was the only way I knew how to live inside the unknown. The twinkling tree lights stayed plugged in long after bedtime, as if hope itself was wired through those strands.

Addie's steroid-fueled outbursts could send us all into chaos, often at 2:00 a.m. She would be wide awake, demanding mum-mums or Sonic tater tots, which of course were nowhere to be found at that hour. Frozen tots were apparently a personal insult. The house became an upside-down world, where day bled into night and sanity into survival. And yet, between the tears and the tantrums, she would look up at me with her beautiful eyes and whisper, "I love our new house." That made the exhaustion bearable.

We began tapering off the steroids. Slowly, our girl was coming back. Her breath, lighter. Her gaze, steadier. We caught moments, fleeting and delicate, of her playing, building towers with Mili or cuddling on her *Frozen* bed, the one my dad painted blue just for her.

Then came *the* night. Her breathing changed. Shallow, rapid, like someone whispering through a straw. We counted each breath, each wheeze, each moment she shifted. Our hospice team came over, quietly acknowledging what we feared: Her body was weak. Her little chest rose slowly and fell heavily. Cody and I camped on the floor next to her *Frozen* bed. I could not close my eyes.

And then, morning.

She coughed, deep, strong coughs. Her breath returned to something that felt almost normal. I whispered a thank you, not knowing who to give it to.

Later, I read a message from a close friend.

Anduin said,

> My heart is heavy. The waiting, hoping, uncertainty; I'm sure you are weary. If we all lived with the passion for life Addie has, the world would be a different place. Give that girl an extra long hug for us; I know you are already pouring everything you have into her, trying to give her enough love for all of us, and all of the missing years. In the end, it may never feel like enough, but please know that you guys have been more than enough. I'm sure that Addie knows how loved she is. I'm so thankful that you proactively took time to make happy deposits in the memory bank. You have treasured this life. Of course, there will never be enough moments; how could there be?

She was right.

My friend Nichelle had written too.

> I was unpacking some books tonight and found Addie's birth announcement Christmas card. Way back then it became my bookmark and it still warms my heart to see her precious dimples in that little pink hat. Love to see those same dimples in every photo you post and memory you share. Thoughts are with you all daily and more!! We love you!

I closed my eyes and kissed those same dimples. Her body was tired, but her spirit was still here.

The social worker said it could happen anytime now. That some children "come back" right before they leave. That they wait for the moment their parents step away. I was not ready for that.

But today, she stayed. Today, we opened another gift.

And today, it felt like Christmas.

The first light of dawn crept through the window, casting a soft glow over the living room. December 20th, 2016, began as so many days had in the past few weeks, with an early morning awakening. But this time, there was a peculiar sense of surrealness in the air, as though the universe itself was holding its breath. Addie was already awake. She always seemed to be awake in the early hours, her body still running on a different schedule. Her days and nights had blurred into one as the cancer in her little body grew stronger.

In her fragile state, Addie asked for her favorite things at the time: PEZ, tater tots, and microwave pizza. She sat at her Minion tray on the couch with Sadie clutched tightly in her hand. The simple act of feeding her felt almost too precious, too delicate, as if these moments of normalcy might slip away without warning. We had learned, over the course of these past few weeks, that each precious minute with her was a gift.

She walked around the house in a dream state, her tiny frame swaying ever so slightly. I could see the exhaustion in her eyes, the battle her body was waging against itself. The cancer in her lungs, stealing her breath; the tumors in her brain, clouding her clarity. But she was still here. She was still with us. There was a sweetness in her presence that made the house feel warmer, even in the depths of winter.

Addie played with Mili that morning, the two of them huddled together over a play kitchen, then smiling over a fish game with a magnetic wand. The joy in her laugh, though faint and distant, was enough to make my heart swell. And as I watched her, I knew something was changing. Something irreversible.

Addie's grandparents left when I knew she needed some rest, and Mili went with them, leaving just Cody and me with our sweet girl. Cody, always the pragmatic one, left for work that morning. I knew he was struggling to face what was ahead. Neither of us wanted to confront the truth that Addie was nearing the end, but we both felt it—deep down, we both knew. We just couldn't say it.

And so, I settled into a routine that seemed both comforting and impossible. Addie curled up in my arms, and for a brief moment, I felt relief. She drifted into a nap. I could breathe for a second. But the clock kept ticking, and the hours stretched on, marking time in ways I wasn't sure I was prepared for.

The house was quiet, too quiet. The air had thickened in the absence of her usual energy, and even the dishes I had meant to wash seemed too heavy to lift. I couldn't rest. Not with her sleeping there, so still. So incredibly still.

A few hours passed, and I watched her chest rise and fall. The gentle rhythm of her breathing was the only thing tethering me to reality. But then, something shifted. Her breath had slowed, and when I gently tried to wake her, there was no response. Panic immediately clawed at my chest. I tried again, calling her name, but the silence was deafening. I felt the overwhelming weight of time, the unspoken dread that had been creeping closer with every passing hour.

I called Cody, but he didn't answer. I left a voicemail. Then I paged him over the speaker at work, my hands trembling as I pressed the buttons. He kept that voicemail, the one I left in desperation, for years after.

Cody rushed home, and when he arrived, there was no way to ignore what we had both been avoiding. Addie was breathing, but her body was unresponsive. We cradled her together, holding her small, limp form between us. We spoke to her, whispered our love, and I could see in her eyes that she could hear us. But she wasn't there. Not fully. Not anymore.

Time felt irrelevant. It stretched endlessly. Our grief alternated between moments of overwhelming sorrow and flashes of joy as memories of her flooded our minds. I remembered her first steps, the sound of her giggle, her bright, contagious smile. And then I would cry, overwhelmed by the love I could never fully articulate, the love that poured from me in waves, even as I was losing her.

The hospice team arrived, their presence a comfort and a haunting reminder that the end was near. We moved her to her *Frozen*-themed bed, the one we had promised her in our new house; a house we had only moved into twelve days ago. It felt so unfair that we hadn't had more time.

We played her favorite storytime song, "Twinkle Twinkle Little Star," because "Let It Go" would have ripped my beating heart right out of my chest. We watched videos on our phone of Addie with the people who loved her most. We waited. We sat with her, offering comfort and love, as her body slowly, steadily, gave way. And then it came, the change in her breathing. The rapid breaths that we had been warned about. And even though the hospice nurse had told us this was normal, I knew.

We spent several more hours with her. The sun set over the Rocky Mountains, casting a serene light through her bedroom window. The sight of that sunset had always brought me peace, but today it was a cruel reminder. Time was slipping through our fingers.

As her breathing became more labored, I knew that the moment was close. I held her tiny hand in mine, feeling the warmth of her skin fading. She blinked her eyes open just before her last breath. In that instant, I felt a quiet knowing pass between us. I wasn't ready, but she was. And in that moment, I felt an overwhelming sense of peace wash over me, a calmness that I would later realize was her letting go, and me with her.

Her last breath came, gentle and soft. And she was gone.

I said to her, in those last moments, everything I wanted to.

The hospice nurse confirmed Addie's death at 10:37 p.m. on December 20th, 2016. Soon after, a black car arrived.

We didn't know what to do next. We were paralyzed by the rawness of the moment. We had made the decision to donate her body to science, hoping that her death could somehow help another child. It didn't make sense, but it did, in a way. She had always been our little warrior, and now, even in death, she was giving.

Thinking about what items to send with her felt like a horrible dream. *Do we want her to have her dandelion blanket, or do we want it? Does she need it where she is going?* It smelled like her, but we wanted her to have it. Still, I held tightly to her favorite comfort item, her stuffed elephant named Sadie, and I could not bear to let it go. It's still in my nightstand for the times I miss her most.

It was almost midnight. I held her one last time, her body soft and weightless in my arms, just as I had done a hundred times before. I could almost hear her voice, already just a memory. "I carry you, Mommy," she used to say to me, always getting the language backward. And as I carried her lifeless body for the very last time outside into the bitter cold, almost falling to my knees, I wondered, *Who will carry me?*

Afterward, the hospice team helped us with the final details of filling out paperwork. They said, "We need to confiscate her pain medication."

I thought, *Why are you bothering us with this task at this moment?* I felt confused and belittled, untrusted. *Do they think I may take those medications to ease my pain right now?* To be honest, they weren't wrong.

And then, they left us alone, just the two of us, empty and numb, in the house that still smelled like her.

We finally had the peace we had been yearning for, but it was the loneliest peace of all.

We tried to distract ourselves, watched a movie, but it was too much. We both fell asleep on the couch, the movie still playing in the background, but neither of us had the strength to wake up.

After Cody and I arose from what felt like an eternal nap, we asked my parents to bring Mili home. She brought her eighteen-month old smile with her, and we hugged her so tightly I thought she might faint from our abundant affection right then and there.

The days following Addie's death brought about a fog of disbelief. Having to pick out a tiny urn, then days later seeing family for Christmas. Gifts arrived addressed to her, and it didn't feel right to open them, though I knew we had to. We didn't know what to tell Mili when her sister was just simply not around anymore. We could tell she knew things were different, but it was all a blur. Addie's freshly painted blue *Frozen* bed was a daily reminder that she was gone from this house. I felt lifeless. For days I went places with Addie's car seat in the car. I knew Mili was confused, but I was not ready to remove it.

Many days, my only goal was to breathe and try to give myself grace, though it was hard. I was so numb from shock it almost felt like denial. With the depth of my despair, the thought of sharing her obituary on Facebook felt cheap. Surely this was all just a dream.

It had been a week without Addie by our sides and somehow it still did not seem real. Christmas had come and gone, and I had no tears to cry. I felt helpless, and I moved through days without any emotion as my initial protection mechanism. All I knew was that I must go on. I had an eighteen-month-old to take care of, and she kept me functioning.

As the year came to a close, I was a spectator in my own life. I could not connect to my environment, and everything else except my grief seemed superficial. I knew "Happy New Year" was not in my vocabulary. I had no idea what 2017 would bring, and no clue how to navigate it. I had no plan except to hold on tight to family and friends in the aftermath.

Dear Addie, thank you for … leaving this world as beautifully as you came.

Adelaide Marie Stiverson

Dec 3rd, 2013 – Dec 20th, 2016

Photo Credit: Flashes of Hope, Lynn Townsend

9

The Year that Wasn't

"While we try to teach our children all about life,
our children teach us what life is all about."

–William Saroyan

I don't remember the beginning of the year. The world spun with its usual rhythm while I hovered somewhere above it, watching it all go by like a film I didn't audition for. That first New Year's after Addie died was a cruel joke. The countdown, the Times Square ball drop and the confetti on TV–none of it made sense. While others were drafting their resolution lists, I wanted to scream at the world, "How can you move on like nothing happened? My daughter just died. Don't you see that?"

The calendar said January. But my body didn't feel it. I was cold, but not from the winter air. It was the kind of cold that came from deep inside–a quiet, suffocating block of ice that numbed everything. I was still parenting Mili, and maybe that saved me, or maybe it buried me deeper in guilt. I often wonder how different my grief would have been if Mili wasn't there. Would our marriage have survived the collapse of our world if it were not for us focusing on parenting Mili? I'll never know. And that's probably for the best.

The days moved on without my consent. My birthday came in March. I turned thirty-eight, and everyone wanted to celebrate me. I tried to smile, tried to show up. But what I really wanted was to disappear. The person they were singing to didn't feel like me anymore.

I missed the hospital. I didn't miss the machines or the chemo protocols, but I missed the people, the nurses who always remembered Addie's favorite foods and movies. I even missed our oncologists, who tried to hide their sorrow behind clipboards. They had been my tribe. And the moment Addie died, they disappeared. Not because they wanted to, but because that's how the system worked. We were handed over like a folder in a filing cabinet. Our hospice social worker got replaced with an unfamiliar grief counselor.

A few weeks after we lost Addie, I wrote thank you cards to our medical team. I didn't know what else to do with the ache in my chest. I needed them to know how much I appreciated them, even though I knew I didn't show it. During treatment I asked so many questions, and I asked them loudly. I advocated for Addie's comfort and demanded answers, and not in a kind way. I was angry, scared, and tired most days. But those cards expressed my truest gratitude. They were love letters thanking the strangers who fought alongside us.

For some strange reason I needed them to know we would be OK after Addie died, though I still wondered if that was true.

I walked those cards into the oncology clinic myself.

The seventh floor. I knew it like my own skin. The scent of alcohol wipes. The sounds and beeps of the IV pumps. I stood at the doorway of that world, holding my envelopes closely. I handed them out in person, not knowing if I was about to collapse or find comfort. It was the first thing I did that felt remotely healing. My voice didn't shake as much as I thought it would. My gracious act didn't bring Addie back, but it brought a small part of me back.

New York Service

At first, I thought I wanted to stay home with Mili. After all, family was everything to me. But every time she invited me to a tea party or to dress up like a fairy princess, I felt as though I was watching through a window. I showed up. I took the photos. But I wasn't there. Not really. And the guilt that came with that was sharp and it cut deep.

I had been there for Addie—through every moment, every treatment, every scan. I was really there. So why couldn't I be fully present for Mili? Why didn't I want to be? Those questions haunted me. But eventually, I offered myself grace. Numbness is a survival tool. And sometimes, survival doesn't look like dancing; it just looks like breathing.

Eventually, I returned to my military work. Not full-time, but enough. I officially transferred to be part-time in the Colorado Air National Guard and promptly accepted an opportunity to serve in a leadership role. It gave me structure and purpose when my heart had none. Cody was still working full-time, carrying us in every way a person could for his family. I hope he knows how grateful I was for that. It gave me time to breathe and time to feel lost.

A few months after I returned to work, we held a memorial for Addie in New York. Long Island was my home. It was my roots, my family, and my childhood. My brother and his family came from Korea for the service, tired from the fourteen-hour trip and the time change, just to be there for us. This was the first time I had seen them since Addie's passing, and I had missed them all dearly. I remembered all the cousins playing together in the months before they left the states—the smiles and pure joy.

The mass was Catholic. Not because I practiced anymore, but because it mattered to my family. And Addie mattered to them. Our cremation decision was hard enough for my family to absorb, so I wanted to bring peace wherever I could.

The church smelled like must and wood polish. I watched as my grandpa cried for the loss of his great-granddaughter, the second one he had lost. I watched the priest, his face filled with sorrow and sympathy. It was beautiful. But I didn't feel it. I felt empty.

Afterward, we drove to the cemetery. There was a small cement box beside the open plot. It was waiting for her. Addie's urn was so tiny, too tiny. We had her ashes split into three urns; one for New York, one for Colorado, and one that would remain in our home. They had all been sitting in a bag from the funeral home, in our closet, for months. This was the first time I took one out.

The burial site was the same plot as her cousin, Alexandra. Alex died four years earlier at twenty-five. She was like a sister to me. Her death was the first one that cracked me open. But this was different. This was my child.

At the grave, we took photos next to Alex's gravestone. This stone would soon have Adelaide's name engraved on it as well, which was hard to imagine through all the floral decor that was placed around it. My aunt handed out candles and people spoke about how Addie touched their lives. I stood there, listening, trying to feel something other than the roar of finality.

The family cleared and only Cody and I remained. We placed the miniature urn in the large box. The void around it made my heart sink with loneliness. We added a letter we had written to her. The silence afterward was louder than any sob. I wanted to snatch her back so desperately. I wanted to keep her in my closet, near me. It didn't feel like peace. It felt like surrender. For the first time since she died, I *had* to let go. It was ugly and necessary at the same time.

We returned to Colorado. We celebrated Mili's second birthday with a *Finding Dory* theme. There were balloons and cupcakes. I took the pictures, but I don't remember much else. Cody turned forty that summer. I barely had the energy to make his traditional yellow cake with chocolate frosting. That year, celebrations were a chore.

We filled our days with our military jobs and spent weekends with friends. But even that felt off. When we went back to Ashlie's house, her son, Everest, asked where Addie was. He missed her, and so did I.

I joined a grief group. We painted memory rocks. I told Addie's story to other bereaved parents. It was strange how good that felt. To speak her name. To be seen. That was when I felt the first spark of something new. I felt ready to connect. I had a new-found hope. I even felt ready to grow our family.

Moving forward isn't betrayal. It's bravery. And my next chapter of bravery was just about to begin.

Weightlessness

I used to love the thought of a nice spa day, just like any mom looking for a break from the chaos of life with children. But after Addie passed away, the idea of a massage no longer felt relaxing; it became an invitation to ruminate on the thoughts I had tried hard to avoid. Silence was my enemy. Yet, somehow, today felt different. I convinced myself that a spa treatment called a "weightless bed" was exactly what I needed.

The advertisement promised to "Reduce mental and physical stress and receive the benefits of a good night's sleep in less than one hour!" It was supposed to release all the musculoskeletal tension in my body, leaving me feeling as weightless as a cloud. *Weightless*, I thought to myself, *now that sounds amazing!* I had been feeling heavy for a while and was desperately seeking a way to relax and feel less stress and anxiety.

Entering the treatment room, I felt a familiar blend of nervousness and anticipation. The lighting was dim, the faint smell of salt-water in the air, and soft piano music playing through a surround sound system. Everything appeared perfectly relaxing, as expected, but the attendant's disposition felt oddly disconnected. Maybe she was having an off day, but her distant attitude felt painfully impersonal on a day when I was hoping for a warm welcome.

I was directed to disrobe and climb onto the platform containing the "bed." Really, it felt more like lying inside a deflated raft than a luxurious spa experience. She wrapped me tightly in thick, plastic material, pinning my arms awkwardly to my sides. Suddenly, I felt trapped. I managed a hesitant smile as she asked if I was comfortable, but before I could voice my concerns, she swiftly left the room. She turned down the music and the lights, commenting that she would return in twenty minutes.

Without any warning, the platform underneath me slowly retracted, leaving me suspended on top of the water floating in silence and darkness. At first, I didn't know what to do with myself or what to feel. It felt awkward and uncomfortable. My body was sinking into the embrace of the warm water, but my arms could not move. They were pinned to my side, like a straitjacket. I felt trapped. My initial confusion quickly turned into overwhelming panic.

As my body experienced the weightlessness, I realized there was nowhere else for me to be but right there in that moment. There was no emergency button to push. I was stuck there, without any awareness of time. And then it happened, tears erupted from a place deep within me, a place I had unknowingly locked away since the moment Addie took her last breath. I was alone with my thoughts for the very first time since Addie died.

In this suspended state, unable to move or wipe my tears, my grief felt unavoidable. With every passing minute, I sank deeper into my own emotional abyss. Images of Addie flooded my mind, beautiful memories wrapped in agonizing sorrow. My tears turned into quiet sobbing; each outburst of emotion was bigger than the last. I was screaming on the inside, pleading for relief. I needed an escape. Twenty minutes had never felt so impossibly long, even longer than the endless eight hours I sat by Addie's bedside as she slipped away from life.

But something strange happened in that suspended space; an invitation to let go came upon me, and a feeling of unexpected freedom engulfed me. There, wrapped in darkness, I had no distractions, no choice but to face what I'd hidden beneath busy schedules, work commitments, and my daily routines. My numbness was being breached. The tightness of the raft felt suffocating, but later became a metaphor for my suppressed feelings. I was trapped physically; yet emotionally, I had finally given myself permission to mourn the loss of my daughter. My heart felt heavy, yet stronger in that moment.

In this weightless moment, clarity emerged. My grief wasn't something I could outsmart, outrun, or ignore. It wasn't something I could neatly organize and resolve in a tidy manner, though I so desperately wanted to. This was a moment of transcendence where my grief felt like the water beneath me, and it was holding me up. It was a surreal experience that part of me didn't want to admit that I desperately needed.

When the attendant returned, my tears had dried up. I felt so different, but her mood remained unchanged. I offered her a genuine smile, knowing the transformation I had just experienced had little to do with her service. It had everything to do with my willingness to embrace my own vulnerability, even just to myself. As I got dressed, I felt lighter, freer, and more peaceful than I had ever felt since Addie's passing.

Grief isn't always loud or obvious. Sometimes, it silently accumulates, hiding behind the mundane tasks of everyday life. Or in my case, on this day, it was hiding just beneath the surface of a floating spa bed experience. Walking away from that spa, I carried with me a newfound respect for the delicate partnership of grief.

Foundation for Addie's Research

I didn't know what legacy really meant until I had to think about it through the lens of a child who wasn't going to live.

There was an ache in my heart—not the kind that makes you cry uncontrollably, but the kind that makes you feel like you should be doing something more. And in the quiet of that ache, I asked myself the same question over and over again: *Now what?* Not the kind of "what's next" that comes with ambition, but the haunting, impossible "what" that comes after something you love so dearly has been ripped away.

I didn't want her to disappear. I couldn't let her just be gone.

So, I started thinking, obsessing on what I felt was an obligation, about how to make her life mean something to the world that kept going on without her. There was no magic moment of clarity, no divine intervention. Just a quiet insistence inside me: *Do something.* I wasn't sure if it was desperation or devotion. Maybe both.

We knew from the very beginning, when we were begging for treatment options that didn't exist, that research for her type of cancer, Hepatoblastoma, was nearly nonexistent. There was only one research foundation remotely dedicated to it, and even that was a drop in an ocean. That helplessness, knowing there was *nothing* new being developed, was its own kind of cruelty. We had good insurance. We had military resources. But we didn't have *hope*, not the kind based in science.

While Addie was still alive, people had reached out and wanted to give: financially, emotionally, and spiritually. At the time, we didn't need the money. But after she died, I remembered every offer. And I knew I would call upon them, not for us, but for the next family. For the next little child with a swollen belly and a tired smile. For the parents pleading with a doctor for something, *anything*, that might work.

A few weeks before Addie passed away, we arranged for her tumor tissue to be harvested. I don't think most people understand how strange it is to plan for a part of your child's body to be shipped off to a research lab. How surreal it is to sign paperwork while still hoping for a miracle. We found a lab that was already studying this disease, an independent non-profit research lab who didn't shy away from impossible problems. That's who we wanted. People who weren't afraid to look at the ugliest truths under a microscope.

Maybe it was for her. Maybe it was for us. Maybe it was just the only thing we could still control. When she was alive, Addie made strangers smile in grocery stores and at the park. She had that kind of rare light that left a true void when it was gone. And I guess I wasn't OK with her light just vanishing.

I wanted the world to care. I wanted someone, somewhere, to look at her cells under a microscope and say, "This matters." I wanted her name to exist in medical journals. I wanted someone to *notice* her. To fight for her, even after she was gone.

Within the first year, we raised nearly $100,000 for that research lab. It happened through continuous efforts contacting people in my network who didn't know what else to do but write a check. And every dollar was a blessing. We partnered with the lab we trusted, the one my mom found when we were still in the trenches. They believed in science the way we believed in Addie–deeply, stubbornly, even when it didn't make sense.

After enough time spent learning, listening, and questioning, I knew I couldn't stop at donations. I wanted to do more than write checks and post on Facebook. I wanted to build something. And so, even though every nerve in my body still ached from grief, I established our own non-profit. I was warned, gently, but clearly by larger, more established foundations that the road ahead would be hard. I didn't need the warning. I was already walking through fire. This just gave me direction.

People didn't always understand. They expected the sobbing, the tears, the shattered woman on the couch watching Netflix shows to drown out my reality. And I was those things, just not in the way the outside world expected. At the time, I called myself a "practical griever." I didn't cry in the grocery store aisles. I pored over cancer research proposals. I didn't scream into pillows. I cold-emailed possible research partners. It didn't mean I wasn't broken. It just meant I didn't know any other way to survive.

And then, the results came back after we had it genetically sequenced. Her tumor–it wasn't even recognizable. There were hundreds of mutations. The researchers said it no longer looked like any Hepatoblastoma they had seen before. I remember staring at the report and thinking, *Of course she was unique. Of course her cancer didn't play by the rules.* Selfishly, I wanted to understand why. I needed someone to explain how this happened. But beneath that was a deeper, quieter hope; that maybe her cancer would teach someone something that could save another child's life.

I dreamed about a future where doctors wouldn't have to guess. Where genetic testing could map out the exact treatment protocol from day one. Where no one would have to sit in a hospital room wondering if the chemo was doing anything at all. Where kids didn't have to be poisoned with the wrong drugs while time slipped away.

And still, beneath all of this science, I just wanted to feel close to her.

We visited the research lab, the one that held her tissue samples. They showed us the nitrogen tanks where they were kept, frozen at negative temperatures colder than anything I had ever known existed. We brought Mili with us. She was only two. She was too young to understand, but I needed her to be there. I needed those photos, even if I wasn't fully present when we took them.

In that moment, standing next to a tank that held the smallest piece of my daughter, I felt her. Not in a supernatural way. Not in some grand, spiritual revelation. Just in the quiet knowing that she was still part of something. Still *doing* something. Even now.

This was just the beginning.

I didn't know what healing was supposed to look like. But I knew it started there, with a little girl's name written into the footnotes of scientific discovery, and a family refusing to let her be forgotten.

An Adoption Story

I always imagined us as a family of four. Not for show, not to meet any social expectation, but because it just felt right. Growing up with

Greg shaped my earliest memories, and I wanted Mili to experience that kind of bond—the wildness, the laughter, the shared glances that only siblings can translate. So after Addie died, when the fog of grief thickened but the outline of that family still hovered somewhere in my mind, I knew we would try again. Not to replace Addie, never that. But to make room for another heartbeat in our home.

At thirty-eight years old, my options were few and laced with fear. I knew the risks of another pregnancy. I also knew I could not emotionally survive another premature birth, or another miscarriage like the one we had before Addie. I first thought of adoption, but when I mentioned this to Cody, I saw he was not ready. He could not speak the word "baby" or "adoption" until after we laid Addie to rest in New York, and Mili turned two. I gave him that time. I needed it too. I had become familiar with the weight of loss, how it settles into your bones before you even realize it has unpacked and plans to stay.

But there was also a quiet whisper growing louder in my soul, and I was ready to feel joy again.

We thought about fostering, a dream I had held for years, but the thought of a child entering and then leaving our lives while Mili was still so young felt unbearable. What I craved was permanence. And what Cody and I quietly hoped for, in the space between conversations, was a baby who would be ours forever.

We began the adoption process with urgency and hope. We were told it could take years, especially since we already had one child, and that many birth mothers preferred first-time parents. But we pressed forward anyway. Time had become our most precious commodity, and we were not about to waste it.

The process was more invasive than I had imagined. We had to open every door of our past, both literally and figuratively. We were peeling back layers of our life: our home, our values, our health, our mental state. We took blood tests, underwent physical exams, and attended an entire weekend of classes. We met with social workers who asked questions that pierced straight through the image of stability we were trying to portray.

During our class, we sat in a small room with two other couples and a single mother, each of us carrying stories stitched with both heartbreak and hope. One couple had mortgaged their home for fertility treatments, only to lose their baby within days. Another had been trying for a child for over a decade, their eyes tired but still holding on to the possibility. A single mother was working toward adopting her second child, and I admired her quiet confidence.

Then there was a same-sex couple who shared, through tears, how they were denied access to the hospital to meet their adopted child because of their race and relationship, an injustice that hung heavy in the air. But the story that reached into my chest and gripped the deepest part of me came from a birth mother. She spoke about how often she thinks of the child she placed for adoption, how the photos and updates were her salvation. I could barely breathe listening to her. It reminded me that adoption is not just about gaining a child, it's about honoring the loss that makes that gain possible.

Could we raise another child so soon after losing one? That was the unspoken question that ran through everyone's minds. But while the world might have seen fragility, I saw something else. A family still standing. A home still filled with love.

Then came the profile creation. A video, a flyer, an online narrative about who we were and what we stood for. I had done online dating before, and this felt strangely similar. Only this time, the stakes were higher. I knew somewhere out there, someone would be flipping through pages of smiling families, looking for a home for their unborn child. I wanted our truth to shine through: our strength, our sorrow, our hope. But how do you tell someone you lost a child to cancer less than a year ago and still make them feel safe choosing you?

We included Addie. We had to. She was part of our family. We also shared our military background, knowing full well that "deployment" could flash like a red warning sign for some. Still, we pressed on. Our profile went live. And then, we waited.

Waiting is not for the faint of heart. Days felt like weeks. I refreshed my email obsessively. We had a few false starts, potential matches that never materialized, and each one chipped away at our already tender hearts.

Then came the call.

I was at home, on the driveway, coloring with sidewalk chalk alongside Mili when my phone rang. Cody was mowing the lawn in the yard. It was the agency. The voice on the other end said a birth mother had found us. She was in her second trimester, she had read our story, and she felt drawn to us. I paused.

"She's having a girl," the woman said.

I caught my breath. I placed my hand over the phone and yelled over the lawnmower, "She's having a girl!"

Cody shut off the mower and looked up, eyes wide and already glistening. He took a slow step toward me, his face breaking into the kind of smile that starts in the heart. He did not say a word, but I felt it—his confirmation.

That was the moment we said yes.

Over the next few months, we got to know the birth mother through phone calls, with the help of our adoption counselors. She had grace in her voice, even strength, and had recently lost her father to liver cancer. The symmetry of our pain connected us in a way that did not need explanation. I believed she loved this baby, and I believed in our love.

We planned, as best we could. The due date was on our calendar—but babies rarely follow plans. A week before her due date, I got the call in the evening around dinner time; she was in labor, and a C-section would be happening soon. Cody was at poker night with his friends, something he rarely ever did. He was at the table going "all-in" on a poker hand when I called. We booked the very next flight. A few hours later, we were on our way.

When we arrived, she had just been born. The moment I held her, I felt an overwhelming rush of joy. I was fully present, emotionally intact for the first time in years. No trauma in my body. No fear creeping behind the moment. Just love. And connection. An undeniable sense that I was made for this baby, and she was made for us.

We named her Emilyn, Emma for short. We gave her Addie's middle name, Marie. Her first name blended her birth mother's name and my middle name, an honoring of the two women who brought her into the world in very different ways. This was divine. This was healing.

We stayed in a hospital room, separate from the birth mother, during the required seventy-two-hour waiting period. Those days felt like walking a tightrope between joy and fear. Any family member of hers could have stepped in and said, "No, we will raise this child." But they did not, even though they seemed extremely capable. They knew she was making the right decision. They came, they met us, they met my parents and Mili, and they saw the love we brought. I believe that mattered.

The goodbye was harder than I expected. We met at a small restaurant. She looked tired, her body still aching from surgery, her chest full of milk meant for a baby she would not nurse. My heart broke in ways I did not expect. I had known the pain of labor. I had known the ache of loss. But never at the same time. In her, I saw both, and I carried both with me.

We hugged. We exchanged gifts. We whispered promises into the quiet space between us. *I will raise her with love. I will not hide this truth from her. I will honor your bravery, always.*

We agreed to an open adoption. I sent photos every month. On her first birthday, I made a photo book for her birth mother. I had a fingerprint necklace made, so she would always know we carried her with us. Years later, we still talk. She has sent pictures of her own childhood, gifts that are priceless to us raising Emma.

There is something about losing a child that changes you at a molecular level. It opens up places in your heart that you did not know existed. You feel more. You love harder. You connect deeper.

Emilyn came to us, not because we deserved her, but because love found a way through brokenness. Her giggles now echo in the same house where grief once lived on every surface. She makes us laugh in the moments we thought would be forever dark.

This is not the end of my grief story. It is still unfolding. But this moment, this chapter, was the beginning of joy returning to my life in the most unexpected, extraordinary way.

Dancing With My Grief

Nearly a year after the loss of Addie, I received a cryptic invitation from my friend Mary, the cancer mom I had met in the hospital.

I wondered what this invitation was about. In the little time we had spent together, she had told me about her career as a dancer, but the registration website was vague at best. A dance show with dinner was all I knew, and I wasn't even sure I wanted to go. I was specifically told to bring a friend. I invited Erin, a friend who was also an accomplished dancer. I pictured us with glasses of wine in our hands watching people move creatively on a stage.

The location was kept secret until just a few hours before the event.

Erin and I arrived at a non-descript residential home in an older neighborhood. We parked on the street a few blocks down, wondering if the GPS led us to the wrong location. Perhaps that added to the intrigue.

This is a strange place for a dance performance, I thought.

The house had extremely small rooms and low ceilings, likely built in the early 1900s. Erin and I walked into the confined space of the entry where we were given several pages of paperwork to fill out.

"How are you feeling today? Describe any recent trauma in your life? What medications are you on? What is your favorite song?"

I felt like I was being screened for an impending psych ward confinement, which didn't seem altogether unrealistic at the time. The fear leading up to the one-year anniversary of my daughter's death was overwhelming.

"What is your favorite song?" I had no idea why this was being asked. I flippantly put down the song swirling around in my head at the time: "Let it Go," from *Frozen.*

Shortly after the intake phase, we were put in a small group of four. I estimated a total of twenty people present for the event, plus the staff. Disappointingly, Erin was not in my group. I wasn't quite sure what was happening.

We were not allowed to talk to the other members of our group. All we were told was that we would experience several stations around the house, and then dinner would be served.

Great. I was already hungry and looking forward to dinner, but I was not prepared for the twists and turns ahead.

Station 1

My first set of directions led me to an old van parked on the street outside the house. Tiny snowflakes began to fall on my cheeks as my group mates and I found our way.

We got in, then intuitively put on the headphones lying on the seats. A video began to play on a TV screen. The video started with a woman, likely in her thirties, dancing on a beach. She was narrating her story about losing her mother to cancer just before having her first child. She reflected on her emotions mothering her children without her own mother.

I suddenly found myself wondering if everyone else around me had been affected by cancer. Was that why I was invited?

Station 2

My next location was the cellar beneath the house. The entrance had a sign saying only one person should proceed at a time. I was first in line. The solid wooden doors were so heavy, I had to use both hands and a hip to leverage it wide enough to slither through. The initial aura in the cellar felt like a horror movie. Then, white lights gave way to a path down the steps to the back corner.

There were no instructions, only a table with supplies to write. Hanging up on a thinly strung line with clothespins, there were handwritten letters. Each note was a personal message, heartfelt notes to people who had passed. They ranged from happy to angry to forlorn to forgiving. After reading them, I sat down at the table.

I wrote my very first message to my daughter: "Dear Adelaide,".... Tears poured down my face, wetting the paper so much I wasn't sure if my writing would be legible to others. I thought of starting my letter over on a dry sheet of paper, but then decided to leave my letter in its authentic state, stained with all my emotion.

I re-read the other heartfelt letters to those who had died, or to people who had been absent. I felt their pain, their joy, their love, and suddenly I felt less alone with the loss of my daughter. It made me realize the weight I carried was a weight so many people carried as well.

Has everyone here experienced a recent loss? Is this why I was asked to attend?

Station 3

I was directed by a staff member to a steep and narrow staircase leading upstairs to a bedroom. There was a baby crib, stuffed animals, and some basic décor. I noticed the contents of an all-too-familiar hospital "go-bag" splayed out on the floor.

A recording started to play when we were all in the room. Mary's pre-recorded voice described, in definitive detail, the anxiety of having to pick up your life in a matter of minutes every time your child with cancer spiked a fever, had a small fall, or simply seemed off. All the memories came flooding back. I could feel my heart racing just hearing the tremble in her voice.

Is everyone here a cancer parent? This must be why I was invited.

Station 4

Next was a tiny kitchen, barely big enough for our small group to stand side by side. Sprawled out on the counter were bottles of pills (represented by candy), liquid medicine (juice), and a list longer than the credits of a Disney movie. Our task was to meticulously measure out each prescription.

At one point, Addie had fourteen different medications multiple times daily. We managed a medication list so detailed and crucial it felt like the cancer was just waiting for us to screw up. This station certainly brought back the daily struggle to stay sane.

At this point in the night, I had not seen Erin at all and began to wonder about her experience. *What was the purpose for bringing her?*

Station 5

The final station was outside, between the house and the garage. It was snowing much harder than earlier in the night. I was ill-prepared for this event for a myriad of reasons, which now included neglecting an appropriate jacket or hat. My body was freezing; between that and the overwhelming memories and emotions, I was weakened almost to the point of collapse.

We circled around a raging campfire so close we shared airspace to breathe. The magical feel of fresh snow resting on my eyelashes diverted my attention from the frigid temperature.

Through individual headphones that were given to us, we listened to all the songs my group put down as our favorite songs in turn. I can't recall any other songs that were played that night, but when "Let It Go" began to play, I could not hold back my tears.

It was the first moment in my grief journey, through my burning eyes and pulsating heartbeat, I felt a true spiritual connection with my daughter. It was foreign yet powerful. Her spirit was with me, holding me up from falling to my knees on the snow-covered ground.

I desperately wanted to let go of the pain, but not the memory of my daughter. I didn't know how to start. The farther away I got from her death, the more it felt like she was slipping away.

That night had fortuitously brought her back to me. I wondered if there would still be dancing. I needed to process my experience, and by now I was starving.

Next was dinner, which was nutritious and delicious—not your typical American portion, but classy enough to get away with it. I was extremely hungry after all the emotional exhaustion, like I had just competed in the "grief Olympics."

Before the dinner plates were abruptly swiped away from our picnic table, eight people, including Mary, slowly entered the single-car garage lit with white holiday lights. The dancers were elegant and beautiful in their movement, positioning themselves around the group. They were dressed in tattered street clothes, which made me feel like they were one of us.

The music began to crescendo in the background and the dancers leaped onto the table with one brisk movement.

I noticed one dancer was holding back tears as she swung from rafters just above me. I don't remember much about the dinner table routine, except that it made me feel joyous after an evening of unplanned self-discovery and deep emotional strain.

I could feel the culmination of stories from the stations coming together around me in their dance. This show was about their most intimate experiences exposed.

At that moment, I felt less alone in the loss of my daughter.

To close out the evening, the dancers performed a stunning group number outside the garage on the driveway while the snow fell endlessly from the sky. There were headlights from a car parked in the driveway shining directly on the dancers.

Their bodies exuded freedom of expression, and their faces were glowing from the snow crystals and lights. The chill in the air gave way to a rhythm I could feel deep inside my bones. I immediately felt lighter, like I was levitating in my seat. Suddenly, I was able to be in the moment and relate to my own journey. I could feel the passion in their movement. I was enveloped in their world and they in mine.

I was truly present with my grief. I felt it so deeply in my soul: the connection, the love.

For a year, I had been mostly numb, filling every minute of my days with tasks for everyone else. The only other time I had experienced such intense grief was in the weightless bed, but this felt like a new level. I would speak of Addie often and tell her story, but was not able to fully connect with my raw emotions surrounding her death. Until now.

After the event, I asked Erin about her experience. She had lost her father to cancer when she was a teenager. This was something I had not known. To say she was deeply impacted by this event would be an understatement.

I'm eternally grateful for Mary, who I met by chance one day on the seventh floor of the hospital. She gave me a gift I could not buy for myself, an unexpected grief experience so profound, it changed the way I connected with my daughter.

December

I used to love December. The twinkling lights, shopping, and the excuse to drink hot cocoa guilt-free on a snowy day. But after Addie's death, December hung in the air like a breath I'd been holding for too long. It was a month full of contradictions, of holiday cheer and heavy shadows. I could hear carols in the background while my own soundtrack was grief, playing on repeat.

It was Addie's birthday month. And now, it was also the month she died.

In less than a year, Mili had gone from younger sister, to only child, to an older sister. We welcomed baby Emma in the fall, and while newborn snuggles came with their own magic, they couldn't smooth the jagged edges of December. Not this one. Not the first.

Cody was angry and I was still mostly numb. Our grief always seemed misaligned. I felt like he had gotten a head start in some ways, grieving before Addie was gone, knowing her time was coming to an end before I did.

I found myself spiraling, trying to figure out what "the first" should look like. The first birthday without her. The first Christmas without her. The first year of surviving something no parent should ever have to survive. I thought maybe I should throw a party. A celebration of Addie's life. A gathering of her little friends at the play place she used to love so much, the same one that brought so much joy on her third birthday.

I booked it. I imagined the laughter, the cupcakes, the bright colors. I thought maybe if we could just remember her smile together, it would somehow feel OK.

As the day got closer, I felt the weight of the event gnawing at me. The idea of celebrating her without her there felt wrong. It felt like putting on a show where the main character was missing. I canceled the booking. I told the gracious owner that I just couldn't do it. He understood even though he didn't have children. Then, I crawled back into the shell I was trying so hard to grow out of.

The pressure to "start a tradition" was unbearable. There's this unspoken rule in grief culture, that on the anniversary, you *do* something. You make meaning. You mark the moment with something significant, something worthy. But all I could feel was fear. I wrestled with fear of doing it wrong. Fear of not honoring her enough. Fear of what the day would feel like and of feeling nothing at all.

The grief books people sent remained untouched, collecting dust on my shelf, except one, *Permission to Mourn* by Tom Zuba. His poetic words met me where I was, drenched in confusion, fighting against every suggestion that implied healing had a checklist. Not only was he a coach and speaker, he had lived through immense loss. "Begin exactly where you are," Tom wrote. I trusted his words, and that line allowed me to stop trying to outrun my own numbness. He also wrote so profoundly, "Grief and pain are the doors we enter to find truth. To create the miracle. To shift our perception, our path to peace and love."[1] At the time, I couldn't quite reach peace, but I held onto the idea that the door was somewhere. And maybe, just maybe, I didn't have to open it yet.

Addie's fourth birthday came and went on December 3rd. Living through the days leading up to it were worse than the actual day. I don't even remember if we had a cake. But I do remember Sonic tater tots, frozen pizza, Doritos, and PEZ. Those were all of Addie's favorites, and surrounding ourselves with those foods felt right. I remember wanting to be alone but also not wanting to disappoint the people who showed up. The grandparents came, and I let them.

I shared her light, even though most of me wanted to keep it all for myself.

Cody's mother made a blanket for me out of Addie and Mili's baby clothes as a gift. It's still one of the most meaningful things I own. Tangible softness stitched together with memories I can no longer hold in my arms.

Earlier that month, the family programs office on base reached out to me about a holiday event. United Airlines was hosting something for families affected by pediatric cancer. Santa, gifts, and a hangar turned into the North Pole. They asked if Mili would like to attend, and I said yes. It felt like a way to hold space for Addie by making magic for Mili. It felt like something I could do for her, though most of the time I felt like these offerings were for others, for people who were struggling.

A few days later, they called back and told me that Mili was too young. There was an age requirement. I didn't argue. I understood. Still, the blow knocked me down a little more that day.

About a week later, I received an email asking for our mailing address. They wanted to send Mili the Santa gift anyway. I wrote back and declined. I asked them to please give it to a family in need. We were OK financially. Others weren't. I wanted to pay forward the kindness that so many had shown us.

December 20th came, the day Addie died. No grand plans. No memorial site yet in Colorado. The two remaining urns were still in my closet. I just needed to survive it, and I did. That day, I gave myself permission to not know. To not "do it right." Because maybe there wasn't a right way.

Christmas loomed next. I did almost nothing. No shopping. No decorating. I found just enough strength to put up a small tree for Mili, which had a special ornament we purchased in the gift shop of the hospital when Addie was born. I dressed Emma in a "Baby's First Christmas" onesie to take a cute photo, and Mili ran around the house in her *Frozen* Elsa nightgown, casting spells. Their joy was the only pulse in an otherwise flat line of a season. Their innocence truly saved me.

On Christmas Eve, the doorbell rang. I was not expecting anyone. A delivery driver stood on the porch with a huge box addressed to us. I had not ordered a single thing. I opened it, alone, standing barefoot near the front door. Inside was a note from the United Airlines program coordinator. They had sent Mili the Santa gifts anyway. They were all wrapped so beautifully; all I had to do was put them under the tree.

I sank to the floor, crying.

Someone who didn't know me, knew. She knew that somehow, a box of wrapped toys on my doorstep could bring light to my darkness. That gesture softened the weight I had been carrying. I didn't need charity; I needed humanity. We didn't need the presents. But I certainly needed the help.

Months later, I told a United Airlines representative our story at a military appreciation event. She cried tears of joy. Sometimes, the smallest acts can reach the deepest places.

I thought December would break me. But instead, it reminded me that sometimes the most unexpected love can arrive in a cardboard box on your doorstep, just when you've forgotten how to ask for it. A stranger's act of kindness didn't erase the pain, but it reminded me that I wasn't completely alone in it. That somehow, the universe was still sending signs that there was light ahead, even when everything felt like it was falling apart.

I didn't have the answers. Not to grief. Not to healing. Not to what came next. But I began to wonder, maybe the answers weren't the point at all. Maybe it was the questions that would lead me forward.

Dear Addie, thank you for ... bringing Emilyn into our lives and guiding me through this year exactly the way it was supposed to be.

10

Questions to the Universe

"The greatest obstacle to discovery is not ignorance—
it is the illusion of knowledge."

—Daniel J. Boorstin

Do you ever wonder if heaven is real?

After my child died, I didn't know what I believed anymore. Somehow the adjacent proximity to death brought a renewed perspective about what it meant to truly live and die on this earth, because everyone will eventually die. I was shaken to my core trying to make sense of anything and everything I had ever known, the things I had always questioned about a spiritual existence.

I was comfortable believing in something bigger than myself, something out there, something gentle and loving that waited for us on the other side. But when your child dies, your belief system unravels like an old sweater. You tug at one thread and suddenly it is just a heap of yarn on the floor.

Everything I thought I knew became a question. I started to study people, the way they responded to death, how their eyes shifted when they offered me comfort. I could tell who believed their words and who recited them like lines from a script. "She is in a better place." That phrase never sat right with me. A better place than in my arms?

No. I never agreed with that. I still do not.

In the fall of 2012, long before I ever imagined I would lose a child, I received a call that cracked the first layer of my protective shell. Cody and I had just finished a cross-country move from Texas to Alaska, our two little dogs nestled in a trailer with us. We took the long way through Canada and Glacier National Park with backroads full of magic and moose sightings. I still remember how we laughed about needing a vacation from our vacation by the end of it.

We were settling into our new home, in the middle of renovating the attic into a bedroom. I was standing upstairs when the phone rang. I picked it up, still in work gloves and covered in sawdust. It was my mom. Her voice gave it away before her words ever did.

She told me twenty-five-year-old Alexandra had died suddenly. Alex, my cousin, the one who was more like a little sister than anything else. We had just been on a cruise with Alex and her new husband, sipping umbrella drinks in our bathing suits, savoring the future of joy and possibilities. She had been thin—a little jaundiced—but smiling.

She died in a hotel room in Texas, alone, during a Starbucks manager conference. Her roommate found her unresponsive. They said it was a diabetic coma. Her skin always bore the story of her illness, but her spirit was bigger than any diagnosis. She had dreams, a new husband, and a future. And just like that, gone.

I collapsed on the unfinished floor.

My family believes in signs—rainbows specifically. When Alex died, everyone began to see them. At first, I tried too. I would scan the skies after rain, but no rainbows came for me. They came for everyone else: my aunt, my mom, even strangers told stories of double rainbows at just the right time. I wanted to believe. I did. But I felt nothing, and that made me angry.

It was not fair. Alex was supposed to be there at my baby shower, at Christmases, at birthdays. She was supposed to watch me become a mom.

Then Addie died in 2016, and everything I thought I had lost with Alex paled in comparison. I was shattered. And yet, a part of me still searched the skies. I did not know what I was looking for anymore. Not a rainbow, maybe not even a sign, just something to hold onto.

In the spring of 2018, my grandpa turned ninety. A good, long life. A kind life. When my mom called and said she didn't think he had much time, I reacted before I even thought about it. My feet were moving before my brain caught up. I booked flights for the whole family: Cody, the girls, and me. I told myself it was to say goodbye to Grandpa.

But it was not.

What I wanted, what I *needed*, was for someone who had known Addie to carry a message to her.

Grandpa had held her when she was sick. He had cried with us. He had felt the kind of heartbreak that skips generations. And somehow, in my mind, I believed he could deliver something across that invisible boundary I could not cross myself. A message. A hug. A whisper. I raced to get there in time.

We missed him by hours.

I did not get to say anything, but something strange happened. I arrived in New York expecting a tidal wave of regret, but instead I felt calm. Not peace exactly—more like an exhale. A release. It was as if he already knew. I pictured him hugging Addie the moment he arrived, sitting down to a plate of spaghetti and meatballs with her in his lap, feeding her bites between stories.

Is that Heaven?

I still do not know. Maybe it is. Maybe Heaven is not a place at all, but a feeling. A flash. A moment when time folds in on itself and you can feel your loved ones breathing beside you even when they are gone.

Every now and then, I catch glimpses. A happy bald child, about Addie's age, wearing a *Frozen* shirt and boots three sizes too big. I melt every time. I want to reach out and hold her, but I never do. I just smile and hope maybe, for a split second, Addie is there.

She shows up in my dreams. She shows up in music, in soft breezes, in silence. I do not need signs anymore, not the way I used to. Now, I just listen.

Some days, I still ask: Will I see her again? Will she still be three-years-old, giggling and holding her Sadie, and waiting for me to play peek-a-boo? What will I look like when we meet again?

I do not have those answers. I do not need them today.

What I do know is that questioning is not a weakness. It is the soul reaching out. So if you are asking questions, keep going. Let your wonder lead you. Let your heart break wide open and ask anyway.

And if there is a Heaven, maybe Addie is saving me a seat.

Or maybe she is everywhere.

Even though a three-year-old lacks a fully developed frontal cortex, just maybe. Addie was wise beyond her years. Maybe she sees my need to help others, and she helps me help them.

The day after Grandpa died, we went to the beach, and the air was crisp in a way that made me grateful to be alive. We watched as the evening orange sun fell through the pink sky till it touched the waving water. Mili picked up a shell and handed it to me with a smile. I looked out over the ocean sunset and imagined a table in the distance with my Grandpa, Alex, and Addie sitting there, laughing, eating, waiting.

Somewhere between belief and disbelief, I found a sliver of peace.

And that was enough for that day.

Ft. Logan Burial

Gravel crunched under the tires as we pulled onto the dirt road in the cemetery. It was early summer in Colorado, the air warm and dry, and the mountain view was glistening in the sunshine. I stared out the window as we pulled up to the tiny sign stuck into the earth like a placeholder for someone who didn't yet belong. Except this time, we belonged. We had chosen to bury Addie's remains in a plot allocated for her and me.

The veteran cemetery felt quiet in a way that wasn't just about sound. It had that hush, the kind that wraps around you when something spiritual is happening. Cody parked the car, and none of us moved for a moment. I looked at the girls in the back seat, small and unaware, babbling about a snack or something they saw on the drive. We had told them we were visiting a "special place for Addie," but they were too young to understand what this moment really meant. Maybe that's why it felt safe, like we could let our guard down, because they wouldn't carry the weight or remember.

We had chosen not to have a service this time. We thought about inviting local friends and family, but then decided we wanted it to be private. A treasured moment. Just us and the wooden box Cody had carved himself, her name etched on the top in a way only a father could: imperfect, uneven, and full of love.

The ground was raw. Literally. Our plot was in a section not yet finished, so instead of grass and order, we were met with dirt, flagged stakes, and a patch of earth that looked more like a construction site than a final resting place. It caught me off guard. I think I expected serenity, not chaos. But then again, what about this journey had been neat and orderly–or expected?

There was a small hole waiting. We could see the small pile of extracted dirt to the side. I dropped down to my knees onto the dusty soil, grounding myself. I thought of New York, of all the people at her first burial and of Alex's spiritual presence there. The only company she had here were veterans much older than her and an empty plot next door for her dad.

My heart felt split between loneliness and serenity. That unsettling feeling of leaving a piece of her behind was there again, but this time it was different. This time, I knew we would be together again. I would be with her one day, and that thought no longer scared me.

We played "Let It Go" from my phone. Mili and Emma twirled in the wind with the kind of careless joy only children have. Cody and I cried. Not in the ugly way we used to, angry and breathless, but in that softer, settled way that still breaks you when the tears fall. It was beautiful, and awful. It was another step forward in our grief that we didn't ask for, but truly needed.

An Ode to Workshops

They say the loss of a child changes your marriage. They say most marriages don't survive. What they don't say is how it rearranges everything you thought you knew about each other. It rips out the foundation, leaves the beams exposed, and hands you a blueprint you can't decipher.

People use the word "disconnected," and it means different things. For Cody and I, it meant most days our grief didn't sync up. When I was climbing out, Cody was sinking deeper. And sometimes it was the reverse. We knew there was still love, but we did not know how to show it. We lacked empathy for each other; it's hard to reach out to help someone when you are also drowning.

I wanted the Gottman workshop to help us reconnect and rebuild. We learned about the "The Sound Relationship House" model. I wanted to believe in it. I wanted to believe in us. It all seemed logical, until it didn't.

We sat in a room with ten other couples. Some were older than us, some younger, some holding hands like they were just strengthening their love, and not fighting for it. I looked at Cody and thought, *Do I even know you anymore? Do you know me? Do we know ourselves?*

One of the first exercises was to answer basic questions about each other. Things like: What's your partner's favorite food? What hobby brings them joy? I sat there staring at the paper in front of me like it was written in a language I had never learned. Cody glanced sideways at me, trying to smile. I didn't smile back. I stood up and left the room.

I sat in the parking lot under a blazing sun and sobbed. The kind of sob that starts in your chest but ends in your stomach. Not holding back tears anymore, I realized that not only could I not answer the questions about Cody, but I couldn't answer them about me. We were supposed to be building a house, but we weren't even on the first level. We were underground in the dark. Six feet under. Just like Addie. That's all I could feel.

Eventually I wiped my face, took a few shaky breaths, and walked back in. We finished the weekend. Barely. The binder from that workshop sat on our office shelf like a joke. A silent reminder that we weren't ready, at least not yet. I was not going to give up, but I didn't know how to make things better.

Later on, I realized that the workshop was intended for stable couples trying to improve their relationship. It shined a spotlight on how shaky ours really was, and how broken we still were as individuals.

Months after that experience, we said yes to another: a personal growth workshop, immersive and intense, recommended by our friends Ashlie and Dan. We didn't even read the full email. We just said yes, because sometimes yes feels easier than continuing to live in the no.

It was one of those workshops that strips everything down. No phones. No distractions. Just long days and longer nights. You sleep in your emotions and wake up with your regrets. And if you're lucky, or maybe just broken enough, you let yourself be cracked open.

And that's what happened. I cracked.

We were asked to dig deep into childhoods and into our pain, into the lies we believed about ourselves. At every break, we were told to call someone important and say what we'd never said. I told people I loved them. I told people I was sorry. I told people the truth.

And then came the grief.

It hit me like a freight train I thought I'd already been run over by. On the second day, I decided to write a letter to Addie. A part of me didn't want to. I was afraid the words would sound hollow, like a postcard from a place you won't go back to. But I wrote it anyway.

There is something about physically writing that feels more validating than just thinking. I told her I missed her, that I still felt her. That I promised not to let her memory fade, even though sometimes it already felt like it was. I told her I was trying. Trying to become the kind of person who could live without her but never forget her.

I stood in front of hundreds of people and read that letter out loud. I could barely see through the tears. But when I looked up, their faces told me I wasn't alone. They *felt* her. For the first time in a long time, new strangers knew she existed. And in some strange, beautiful way, she was back.

Ashlie and Dan were there, too, crying beside Cody and me. They had all watched the moment I stopped hiding her behind closed doors. The moment I let her live outside of me. It was agony and relief all at once.

Afterward, I walked outside and looked up at the sky. I didn't feel fixed. But I felt more *present* than ever before. And maybe, that was enough.

A few weeks later, at a grief conference hosted by the children's hospital, I raised my hand to speak to other bereaved parents. Not because I had answers, but because I had *questions*. And sometimes that's more important.

What does grief really look like? Is there a prescribed path or a timeline?

I told them about the workshop. About the letter. About how it hurt and healed and hurt again. I told them it was OK to be wherever they were. That sometimes grief looked like progress, and sometimes it looked like crying in a Target parking lot for no reason at all.

I spoke my truth. And that mattered.

I started wondering, *What if parents like me, bereaved, broken, aching, could be empowered by their loss?*

What if this pain didn't just destroy us, but remade us? What if?

I wrote that question down in my journal like a dare to the universe.

I was finding pieces of myself again. Not whole, not yet. But glimmers. Slivers. And that was more than I had before.

I was above water. Still breathing.

Still holding on to the letter, and my questions.

Nothing Left

I was making progress along my grief journey, but there was one trigger question that always brought me back to my reality: How many children do you have?

It's a question that usually comes naturally, casually, and innocently from well-meaning strangers. Other moms at the library or parents at the park. Even a cashier making polite conversation as she rings up my toddler's yogurt bites. In fact, it's a question I used to ask other parents too.

Now, it feels like stepping on a landmine every time I hear it. Answering this question feels torturous to me.

Some days, I would say two, Emma and Mili. I have two little girls, here, alive, and breathing. They are the ones I see in front of me. I brush their hair, tie their shoes, and sing goodnight lullabies to them. They are here with me. But when I say two, I feel a betrayal. I feel Addie's absence in the silence her name should have filled. She is also with me.

Other days, I say three. I brace for the follow-up questions: ages, schools, the inevitable curiosity. I swallow the lump in my throat and try to say it without too much emotion. *I'm a mother to three girls. My oldest, Addie, passed away from cancer when she was three.*

The words drop like boulders in a river, heavy and uninvited. The reactions I receive are always the same, startled eyes with quiet gasps, and then an awkward backpedaling of well-intentioned sympathy.

Oh my gosh, I'm so sorry. I can't imagine anything worse.

Yeah. I can't either.

It's the pause that follows that hurts the most. Like the world doesn't know what to do with me anymore. Like I just broke some unspoken parenting code by bringing death into the conversation. I didn't choose this. I didn't ask for this story.

And still, it's mine.

Every single time, it sucked the energy out of me. I had no go-to response. I had not figured out how to package my reality into a socially acceptable soundbite. All I had was this internal battle of despair that kept playing on repeat in my mind.

Will I ever see this person again? Do I want to share my story right now? Would it even help if I did? Have they ever met anyone whose child had cancer?

Eventually, I started withdrawing from places where I might have to answer this dreaded question. I would skip the playdate or the birthday party. I would bypass any eye contact in the grocery store. I would rush out of the library right after storytime. I avoided small talk altogether. It was just too exhausting. But grief doesn't disappear when you avoid it. It waits. It seeps in through the cracks and moments of silence.

For a while, I tried to pretend everything was fine. I wore a fake smile, when just beneath the surface I was a total mess. I drank more than I used to, even though alcohol was never my thing. I showed up for some things to save face and made crafts with the girls to feel normal. I even laughed sometimes. But under all of that, I was unraveling.

I wondered if this was how rock bottom felt? This relentless questioning of my reality along with an aching and constant internal struggle. Many people say you need to hit the bottom before you can rise back up. But how would I know if I was there? I was always waiting for it.

And then one day, the bottom found me.

I was alone, driving my minivan down a familiar Colorado highway. It was bright, clear, and the road stretched endlessly ahead. It didn't care about my suffering. Images raced through my head, as they often did—swerving sharply, crashing into a ditch or flipping the car spectacularly. It played out like an epic scene from a movie. Visions of a hospital room, my family standing over my broken and lifeless body. These thoughts flooded my mind with chilling clarity.

Then, without consciously deciding, I jerked the wheel.

My heart raced as my minivan skidded onto the gravel shoulder, dust clouding my windows. The brakes screeched to a halt. I was driving at least ten miles over the 75 mile per hour speed limit; because that's what you do when you just don't care. The car stopped, time stopped, and the numbness I had been fighting against since Addie took her last breath swallowed me whole.

I sobbed so hard my whole body shook. I couldn't breathe; the weight of the grief I had kept hidden even from myself was so heavy. I felt like I was disintegrating right there on the side of the road. I wanted someone, anyone, to see me, to care. I wanted to hear, "You're not crazy. Your child died and you are allowed to feel this way."

But no one did. It was just me.

That was the moment I realized I couldn't get any lower. I had tried to scare myself into feeling something. And it worked. I felt terrified and not just of the road.

I was afraid I might disappear while still living. I was afraid I would miss everything I was put on this earth to do. I was afraid my girls would lose their mother. And I knew, no matter how deep the pain, I couldn't do that to them.

Whether I had been suicidal or just desperate to be seen didn't matter. That was my wake-up call.

In the stillness of that painful clarity, something shifted inside me. This wasn't fair, not to my girls, not to my family, not to myself. I knew I had to care for myself, because no one else could heal these wounds. I had to find a way to be truly present, not just physically, but emotionally too.

I had to claw my way back out of the ditch. I didn't know how. I just knew I needed to try. I still had moments of dissociation, moments where I was physically there but emotionally gone. I took photos I don't remember. I planned parties I can't recall. I made a smash cake for Emma's first birthday. I danced with Mili in mommy-and-me class. I dressed the girls in tutus and princess dresses. It was magical for everyone watching me.

But inside, I knew I wasn't present. And I hated it.

And so, I began. I started with running.

It wasn't pretty. I was out of shape, and my lungs would burn, but I needed to work my way back to a person who resembled me. To not be needed by anyone for thirty minutes. To move my body and feel the physical challenge of breathing in the cold air.

Running was never about love for me. It was about survival. First it was to pass my military fitness tests. Then it was to prepare for something harder: a triathlon, a summit, a race that needed grit. But in my forties, running transformed into something else. A place. A ritual. A return.

Grief made me run. Not in the poetic sense. I mean it literally made me get out of the house and run until my lungs burned and my thoughts slowed. Some days I ran so hard it felt like I could outrun the pain. But of course, it always caught up to me. Somewhere between mile two and three, it would settle in beside me like an old companion. I stopped resisting. I let it run with me.

I do not chase the runner's high. I chase serenity. A moment when the noise fades and I can hear my own breath. The trails near my house are familiar now. I know every bend, every tree root, every incline. But the strange thing is, it never gets old. The light changes. The air shifts. The leaves fall and grow back. Some days there is snow. Just like grief, the landscape is the same, but I am not.

I listened to the same song every run, for three miles on repeat. "I Am Here," by P!nk. It became my anthem. The lyrics played over and over as my feet pounded the pavement.

And I began to believe them in my soul.

Some days, I couldn't even run the first mile. Other days, I ran until my legs ached, even more than three. Whatever happened, every time I put on my shoes, I was choosing to live. To heal. To show up. To take care of me for the first time in a long time.

This practice, of movement, of rhythm, of listening, had become my church. I did not preach it. I lived it. And somehow, that felt like enough.

Rachel Platten's voice in her song "Better Place" became my cool-down sob, and I began to ask better questions—not of others, but of myself.

How do I want to remember Addie? How do I want to live for Emma and Mili? How can I live fully and be present, even with a gaping hole in my heart?

I didn't find all the answers. But I found myself.

And maybe that's the point. Because sometimes, the questions are enough. They don't erase your pain; they shape it.

I am here. The world *is* a better place because of Addie.

And this isn't the end. Not even close.

Lessons From the Dying

I took a death class.

That is how I usually start the sentence, just to watch people squirm a little. I don't say it for shock value, though it does tend to grab attention. I say it because it is the truth. I sat in a Zoom room with a handful of acquaintances, led by my friend Rachael, who became a certified death doula after losing her son Henry. We met at the Children's Hospital grief group. Together, we talked about dying.

The purpose of the class was not to relive my daughter's death. I could not stomach that. It was to explore my own. And not in a poetic, abstract way, but in a very real, down-to-the-last-detail sort of way. As if I had been told I only had three months to live. Or, in my case, maybe three minutes. That felt more honest. Sudden death felt more aligned with my recent thoughts, and somehow, easier to imagine.

After Addie died, the world became louder. Airplanes felt more dangerous. Fevers were no longer innocent. I hovered over my other children like a rescue helicopter, ready to drop in at the first sign of trouble. I could not tell if I was grieving or panicking.

Maybe both. Probably both. I was afraid of dying, and I was terrified of not truly living. This class helped me through both.

In this death class, we were guided through five domains: Mental, Practical, Emotional, Physical, and Spiritual. That might sound tidy on paper, but it was not. Each domain was like a dusty drawer in my soul I had forgotten existed, and opening them required more courage than I expected.

Mental Domain

We were asked what we were most proud of in our lives. What gave our life meaning? I froze. I stared at the question as if it was written in a language I used to know. Slowly, I began to write: my children, my marriage, my military service, and Addie's legacy. It came out like a whisper at first. Then louder.

I next wrote about how I want to be remembered. Not for what I accomplished, but for how I made people feel. That I was kind. That I was steady, even when I was shaking inside.

Practical Domain

This was more straightforward, at least on the surface. As military veterans, Cody and I already had a will. We had some plans in place. But this class pushed me further.

Where are your documents stored? Who gets the sentimental items? What do you want done with your body?

That last one landed with weight. I had to pause and consider it, really consider it. I decided I wanted to be an organ donor. If I could help someone else live, just like Addie's donor had done for us, I wanted to. And if science could benefit from what was left, then let them have it. We made this decision for Addie and now I would get to make my own.

I wrote down that I wanted a celebration of life, not a funeral. No black outfits. No platitudes. I pictured people gathering, smiling through tears, remembering who I truly was. I want gratitude in the room. I want people to feel that I lived with purpose, even when I was lost.

Emotional Domain

This was the hardest.

Writing thank you messages to the people I loved felt like peeling off layers of armor I did not know I still wore. I could not yet bring myself to write letters to our girls. That broke me. I tried, but the words would not come. Instead, I wrote short love notes. I left pieces of me in journals, tucked away in pages they might someday read. I promised myself, if I ever got the gift of knowing I was dying, with time to prepare, I would write those letters. I would not leave without telling them everything.

Others in the class had relationships they needed to heal. Watching their courage moved me. Not everyone gets a second chance, but we can choose not to wait until it is too late.

Physical Domain

This domain asked us to imagine our final days. Not metaphorically. Literally. Where would I want to be? Who would I want there?

I closed my eyes and saw the Rocky Mountains. My family. My girls. A fireplace. Quiet. I imagined holding Addie's hand again. Maybe not here. Maybe somewhere beyond, but that was enough for me.

Imagining this was so powerful. And yet, these are things we never talk about. Not with the people we love most. Not until it is too late.

Spiritual Domain

This one took the most time. I do not know what comes after this life. I hope there is something. I hope Addie is there, peaceful and pain-free. I hope she is with my grandparents, my cousin, and the military friends we lost too soon. I hope the air is fresh and the colors are brighter than I have ever seen.

I do not believe everything happens for a reason. That feels dishonest. But I do believe what we do with what happens can give it meaning. I believe in legacy. I believe in leaving something better behind. I believe we are here to love, to learn, to grow, and then to let go.

By the end of the course, I had created a document I called my "Legacy of Life." It held my wishes, my memories, my hopes, and even my fears. When I printed it, I felt weightless.

Not because I was ready to die. But because I was finally ready to live.

I had faced the very thing most people run from, and it did not break me. In fact, it built me. Stronger. Calmer. More aware. My gratitude was no longer something I had to find. It was something I carried with me every single day.

If you have never taken a death class, maybe you should. Not because you are dying, but because you are not.

What if you could live each day to the fullest, without fear of dying? Would you live differently if you felt truly free?

Dear Addie, thank you for ... teaching me about life through death and for showing me the bottom I couldn't find, so I could rise up to be the person I couldn't see.

11

To Be Unbroken

"There are no shortcuts to any place worth going."

—Beverly Sills

In the isolation of the pandemic lockdown, amidst the uncertainty that surrounded all of us, I stumbled upon a transformative concept during a seminar I attended. The virtual event was hosted by Tony Robbins, a man widely known as the nation's top life and business strategist. I had heard his name referenced many times by people I knew, but this was the first time I committed to one of his workshops.

There were many take-aways from my experience, but one specific sentence he said hit me deep in my core. "If you want to change your life, figure out how your worst day was your best day." Initially, the idea felt impossible, almost offensive. How could the deepest pain, the most unimaginable loss, ever be seen through the lens of gratitude or pride?

It was a challenge, an invitation to gently revisit the hardest moments of my life, not to relive the pain but to uncover the strength, love, and beauty hidden beneath the surface. And so began my journey toward reframing my greatest heartbreak. I was committed to finding clarity, understanding, and ultimately, freedom.

Addie took her final breath on December 20th, 2016, in her *Frozen*-themed toddler bed. As devastating as this moment was, it was also deeply profound and life-changing. The hospice team's gentle yet firm guidance provided me with the strength and clarity I never imagined I possessed. Their compassion and expertise taught me something essential: courage doesn't always come in moments of triumph; sometimes, it emerges quietly in our most vulnerable and painful experiences.

Before I had the hospice team, I never even thought of what her death would be like. I remember hearing it so clearly: "Do you prefer to be home or in the hospital when she passes away?" And just like the shock of her diagnosis, time stood still, and in that moment my body felt completely numb. I had not thought about it like it was a choice. We had been through so many tough calls in the hospital with chemotherapy, surgeries, code blues, and seizures, how would I even know what to do for her at home? I was not a nurse. With nearly everything in my life prior to becoming a mother, I could visualize my achievement before it happened, but this was the first time I truly doubted myself on a whole new level.

I feel privileged to have had an amazing hospice team coach me along the way, as many people don't get that opportunity. The nurses made what felt impossible, possible; they gave me the unwavering strength to help my dearest Addie pass away peacefully at home, in her own bed. It was no secret she was going to die, though up until the moment her breath stopped, I still believed in miracles. The moment she closed her eyes for the last time was excruciatingly painful and truly beautiful all at the same time.

I take that proud moment of helping my daughter die peacefully at home—where I did what I didn't think was possible—with me in my heart daily; along with my gratitude for the three years and seventeen days she was here with us, and the lifetime of inspiration she will bring. That's how the worst day of my life was also my best day. I have transformed my life around this thought. Now, I feel free from the burden of pain and can soak up the glory of her love each and every day.

I remember asking the hospice nurse the night Addie died, "How can you do this day in and day out? How can you watch children die over and over?" The answer she gave didn't resonate till the moment I relived it. She said that she felt privileged to be able to help parents in their darkest moments. It was how she found purpose.

This transformative realization reshaped my perspective entirely. The beauty in the moments were much more clear this time. The hospice nurse that helped me that night gave me a gift I could not give myself.

I began to see that day not only as one of immense loss, but also as my proudest moment; a moment of eternal love and enduring strength. The pain of her passing was undeniable, but so was the pride in knowing I had given her a peaceful and dignified departure from this world.

With the hospice nurse's guidance and constant support, I found courage within myself that surpassed any recognition or medal I had received during my military career. It became clear to me that helping Addie pass away peacefully at home was the most courageous and meaningful act of my life so far.

Unspoken Goodbye

In the first few years after Addie's death, my mother's grief was palpable. It was overwhelming, raw, and filled with so many layers of pain that I couldn't fully comprehend them. My mom had a bond with Addie that was indescribable, and as a grandmother, she had so many hopes and dreams for her, just as I did as her mother. But there was one thing that haunted my mom in particular; she never got the chance to say goodbye in person.

When Addie fell asleep one final time, my mother called and asked to come over. Her request was filled with aching sincerity, a grandmother desperate to hold her granddaughter just one more time. Yet, Cody and I made the painful decision to deny her this moment. We craved privacy, quiet intimacy, an ending shaped only by our love. We had spent much of the year feeling guided by everyone but ourselves, and in this final moment, we wanted it to be ours alone. We gently but firmly declined my mother's request.

I had no idea how heavily this decision would weigh on my mother or how deeply it had wounded her. For years, she silently carried a quiet resentment, particularly toward Cody. She believed it had been solely his choice to keep her from Addie's side. In truth, while Cody had initially expressed this preference strongly, we ultimately stood united in our decision.

Regardless, my mother's grief was different from mine. Hers included not just the pain of losing a granddaughter, but also the deep ache of missing that moment of closure she desperately sought.

Eventually, my mom and I sat down together at a quiet brunch, a moment long overdue. Her voice shook and her eyes glistened with tears as she spoke of that painful memory, the denial of a final touch she believed she needed. My heart sank beneath the weight of guilt, a heaviness that had grown significantly over the years. I realized how deeply this had hurt her, how the absence of that goodbye felt like an unspoken dismissal of her love.

Months later during a moment of reflection, deep in a meditative state, I allowed myself to fully relive that painful interaction. In this quiet space, clarity emerged. I saw the moment I told my mom "no" from a divine perspective, recognizing profoundly that it happened exactly as it was meant to. Addie's spirit was not bound by a final physical goodbye; her love was infinite, transcending that moment.

When I later shared this revelation with my mother, she responded, not with bitterness, but with a quiet, knowing acceptance. Together, we found peace, an unspoken understanding blossoming between us, releasing the heavy burden we both had carried. Our shared grief was retold, reframed, and rewritten. It evolved into a bond forged in understanding and renewed love. My mother began to embrace a deeper truth, that Addie's spirit remained vibrantly alive within us both, unhindered by the absence of a physical goodbye.

Four years after losing Addie, to the month, something remarkable shifted within me. For the first time, I felt no crippling headaches, the ones which used to find me every day of December. My body and soul felt wonderfully alive. This transformation was purposeful and hard-earned, rooted deeply in my commitment to reframing my worst day and the guilt I carried for my mother's unspoken goodbye.

The tangible awareness that your child has died never goes away, but grief can change.

My daughter died, and I will live but not with the pain of losing a child.

Addie taught me how to truly feel alive. Every day is a testament to the love she left behind, a love far more powerful than any final goodbye.

As I step forward into this new identity, I wonder about you and your story. What would your grief look like if you could find beauty in your deepest pain?

Picture On My Desk

Light streamed through the blinds in my new office that morning. It was one of those quiet, unassuming days that marks the beginning of something life-altering, though you don't know it at the time. It felt like I had walked onto a stage I no longer belonged to, reciting lines from a life I was no longer living. My body had returned to work, but my heart hadn't caught up.

I had walked into my new office like a stranger in someone else's life. Only a few months had passed since Addie died, and I said yes to a temporary leadership opportunity. I needed something, *something* to bring me back to how I knew myself, even if I was an empty shell. I was asked to serve on the homefront for a year, backfilling a deployed commander. I brought only one personal item with me to the office—a framed photo of my family, taken in the last sliver of time before cancer entered our world. Addie was two. Her smile in that photo was wide and pure, the kind that makes your eyes squint and your heart squeeze. I placed it on the corner of my desk, facing out.

That was it. That was all I allowed myself.

I focused on the mission. It was easier that way. The structure of military life gave me somewhere to place my hands, somewhere to anchor my feet, while the grief hollowed me from the inside. I told no one about her. Most of my team didn't know I had recently buried my child's ashes. I told myself it was professional to keep it private. I convinced myself grief would make me appear weak. Unfit. Too emotional.

People would glance at the photo on my desk and say, "What a beautiful family you have."

I would nod. Smile. Ask them about their own kids, all the while, crumbling.

Looking back, I know now what I did not know then: I missed a chance to connect. I missed a hundred small chances. I thought I was protecting myself, but really, I was sealing myself in a glass case. From the outside, I looked polished and composed. Inside, I was drowning.

It took six months for the ache to become unbearable.

One morning, I just stared at the photo. At her. And I asked myself, *Who am I protecting?* The answer came in a whisper. I was protecting myself from the pain of saying her name out loud. From the fear of breaking open in front of others. From the risk of being seen in my sorrow.

But grief isn't weakness. It's love with nowhere to go. It's the space she used to fill. When I finally told my team, I didn't have a speech. I just told them the truth in a staff meeting. I told them about Addie. I told them I was not OK, but I was still here.

The next day, one of my team members came into my office. She sat down and quietly told me she had been struggling with infertility and multiple miscarriages. I listened. I understood. In that moment, the air between us changed. We were no longer two women at work. We were two mothers, sharing loss, and something new began to grow in that space. It was real. It was honest. It was human.

Emma, with only a few years under her belt, used to say, "Sharing is caring, Mommy." She meant it when she offered a bite of her snack or a hug at bedtime. But now I know how deeply true those words are. Sharing your story might feel like breaking, but it is often how we care. It is often how we begin to heal.

That moment was the beginning of my return, not just to work, but to myself. A different self. A more vulnerable leader. A woman who could hold the weight of grief and still reach for connection.

Grief did not make me less of a military leader; it made me more human. More open. More empathetic. More real. And by being real, I gave others permission to be too.

The picture still sits on my desk, a quiet witness to the life we had. But healing has many forms, and not all of them sit still. One day, I realized it was time to create a new image, a new chapter. One that honored what we lost, but also reflected what we'd become.

I had been avoiding a new family photo shoot for just over four years since Addie died. The idea felt impossible. How do you take a photo of a family that's missing someone? But I knew it was time. Not just for me, but for Emma. This was her family. A family that started after her sister had already gone. She deserved to be seen, not just as an addition, but as someone who completed us.

I was scared. Scared of what it would feel like to stand there without Addie. Scared of how it would show up in the photos, in the awkwardness behind my smile. A mother in grief once told me to bring something that represents your child into the photo. Something just for you.

So I chose Addie's purple blanket, the one hand-knitted by our neighbor in Alaska, the one swaddled around her as a newborn. We wrapped it around Mili in this photo, as the wind whipped our hair into our faces. Emma wore a sweater I had once knitted for Addie, but she had never worn. It was a renewal of something divine. A thread from the past woven into our present.

To the outside world, we looked like an ordinary family of four. But we knew.

We knew what that photo held. The softness of the blanket, the wind on our faces, the weight of what we survived. We took pictures of the girls running and laughing in the background while Cody and I sat still, holding each other. Capturing, without saying it, the truth that we made it through something unthinkable, and we were still together.

That photo sits next to the old one now. Both belong. Both tell the truth. One of what we had. One of who we are now.

This is what healing looks like. Not perfect. Not complete. But whole, in a different way.

Black Sheep Values

It was not a lightning bolt moment. It was more like a whisper in a room so quiet, I could finally hear myself think.

I was sitting in the back row of a pediatric cancer conference, a gathering where the people all wear familiar expressions of both hope and hurt, and you cannot tell which one is stronger. I was invited to attend that conference two and a half years after Addie's passing. At the time, I was questioning everything and had just hit rock bottom. I was not looking for a miracle, but for something–anything–that would help me breathe again without my chest aching.

That was when Brant Menswar walked on stage and introduced himself, not just as a speaker, but as a father whose child had survived cancer.

I wanted to be moved. I wanted to feel grateful. I wanted to feel inspired by his story of his son's, Theo's, survival. And I was. But in the depths of my own grief, it felt like trying to find a heartbeat underwater. His child lived. Mine did not.

But then, he said something that landed hard.

"I want to tell you about 'black sheep values.' A black sheep's wool cannot be dyed. It is one hundred percent authentic, just like your values. They are the part of you that cannot be changed, no matter what happens to you."

I wrote that sentence down, slowly, deliberately. What were my unchangeable values? What were the things I could not unfeel, unlearn, or unlove, even after Addie died? That was the question I left with. I carried it like a coin in my pocket, touching it over and over again in the quiet moments to make sure it was still there.

The answer did not come easily. I sat with it for months. My grief had rearranged me, cracked me wide open, and left only the most essential parts. I questioned everything. Was I still the same person? Did anything still matter?

I kept digging.

When I finally found my values, I cried. Not because they surprised me, but because they did not. They had always been there, the beams of a house I did not know was holding me up. They were truths. They were me.

I printed them out and taped them to the inside of my closet. Right next to the hand-crafted cards from my girls, these five words are the compass I reach for when I forget where I am going. On the days when the sadness creeps in quietly, when I hold Addie's stuffed Sadie and look at her tiny pink Crocs that no longer have an owner, I glance up and remember: I can still live by what matters. Family. Connection. Perseverance. Impact. Gratitude.

Each morning, I choose which one to focus on first, though I need them all. Some days I lean into connection and call someone just to hear their voice. Some days it is perseverance and I show up to teach my cycle class even when my body aches with exhaustion. Other days it is simply gratitude—for sunlight, for breath, for my girls' giggles, for the fact that I am still here.

Living into my values everyday did not bring my daughter back. But it brought *me* back.

I am still me. Just redefined.

And what I did not know then, was that this tiny act of choosing my values every day would lead me to something even bigger, something I never thought possible again.

The beginning of my transformation.

Grief In My Days

I never thought I would get a tattoo. I had always associated them with college parties, bold rebellion, or deeply personal stories I could not quite understand. But one day, I sat across a woman in my grief group and watched her trace the outline of her child's name on her wrist. It was quiet, simple, and intentional. That was the first moment I knew I wanted one too. Not as a decoration, not as a statement, but as something permanent. A quiet whisper on my skin that says she was here. That she mattered. That she still matters.

I did not want her portrait on my back or a heartbeat line across my forearm. I wanted something softer. Something that spoke to me. A blowing dandelion, scattered across the top of my foot. Her name, *Adelaide*, nestled delicately in the stem. Addie loved dandelions. Maybe she still does. I can still see her tiny hand plucking the white fluff, her cheeks full of air, and then that joyful exhale as the seeds scattered into the breeze. Each time she blew, I wished. For her. For me. For something I could not name. The wish never had a shape, only a feeling, like hope wrapped in a heavy fog.

Now, when I lace up my shoes, I see her name. It anchors me. Some days it is the reason I keep going. I can show it when I want to share her story. I can hide it when I need her all to myself. On those days, she is mine again. My Addie. My light.

There was a time when stillness frightened me more than physical pain. Meditation was a foreign language I refused to learn. I thought silence would swallow me. But loss shifts the rules.

I tried six meditation apps before I found something that made sense to me. Tony Robbins called it *priming*. I called it survival. I committed to his voice for thirteen minutes each morning at 5:00 a.m. for twenty-one days, hoping something might shift. And it did. I created a habit.

Each morning I sat still and tried to remember who I was beneath the grief. I began with quick, strong breaths, pumping my arms, demanding my body to wake up. Then I searched for three moments of true gratitude. Not the kind people post online, but the small truths that kept me tethered to life. The fact that my legs could still run. The echo of Addie's giggle in the back of my mind. The marriage that Cody and I still had.

I let memories of joy rise inside me until I could almost feel light moving through my chest. I imagined sending that light toward the people I loved, hoping it would reach them. Then I pictured myself moving forward, a clear vision of who I would become. I saw myself laughing again, even if it was through tears. I saw myself building a life that had space for both pain and beauty.

And here I am. Not healed, but whole in a different way. Not finished, but no longer stuck.

Now, every morning, even if just for one minute, I start again. Some days are chaotic, some are calm, but my mind remembers. It knows the way back to center. Grief still walks beside me, but I am no longer afraid of its shadow. We move together now. We are partners. It is no longer the thing that happened to me. It is part of my life that is happening for me. I realized I was emerging as someone new. Someone I had not met yet. Someone Addie would be proud of.

But I wasn't the only one changing.

Around that same time, Cody retired from the military, the life he had known for over two decades. He never went back to being a pilot after Addie died, vaguely telling me it just wasn't for him anymore.

We had a small ceremony toward the end of the pandemic to commemorate his achievement. On the surface, it looked like a quiet career ending. But underneath, something much heavier was shifting.

For over four years, he had carried my voicemail from the day Addie died. It was saved on his office phone, tucked away like a time capsule. He never shared it with anyone, never talked about it much, but I knew it was there. My voice—unfiltered, untouched by time—was his tether to the last moment before the world tilted. He listened to it often. It brought her back, even just for a few seconds. And then he'd go back to work. Go back to breathing. Go back to holding it all together.

On his last day in uniform, he deleted the voicemail.

Later that night, he told me quietly, "Retiring wasn't the hardest part. Letting go of that moment right before, that's what broke me."

I didn't need to say anything. I just reached for his hand, because I understood. Letting go doesn't always look like a big release. Sometimes, it's the quietest grief that cuts the deepest.

We were both shedding old versions of ourselves, parts we had clung to out of love, fear, and memory. Not to forget, but to make room for whatever came next.

And when I finally stepped forward, toward that bridge I had not been able to cross before, I carried his story with me too—because it was our story.

And it was time.

The Bridge

It took years before I realized I had crossed a bridge. Not metaphorically. Viscerally. I could see it. Rope and wooden planks, the kind Indiana Jones would hesitate to cross. Beneath me, a crevasse so deep I could not see the bottom. For the longest time, I clung to the frayed edges of that bridge. Most days, I questioned if it would hold. Some days I would let go just a little. Other days I crawled, inch by inch, palms bloodied with splinters.

But eventually, I stood. Cautiously. I took steps forward. And eventually, I crossed.

Now, the bridge has collapsed behind me. I can no longer return to the place where my bones ached to simply survive the day. I do not want to go back. The ground beneath me now is not steady because grief disappeared; it is steady because I have built it plank by plank, using what I carried with me. I did not know I had the tools until I used them. I did not know I would live again, until I did.

That was what acceptance felt like for me. Not like peace. Not like closure. But like gravity finally relenting just enough to let me breathe. People used to say to me, "I cannot imagine anything worse than losing a child." For a long time, I agreed. I could not either.

But I can now. I can imagine two outcomes that would be worse.

One: if Addie had never come into our lives. If I had never gotten to feel her warm head against my chest, never memorized the shape of her smile, never seen her light shine so bright it reached others. That would be worse.

And two: if I had let her death be the end of my story. If I had let the pain define me, mold me into someone brittle and distant. If I had let the most beautiful chapter of my life be followed by blank pages. That would be worse. Not fully living my life.

Pain never left. But it lost its place in the front seat. I began to value something more than my agony. I began to value her life. I began to value mine. When I shifted my thoughts to what I had, even for a moment, I had already won.

I used to see hospital beds and vomiting and fear when I thought about Addie's cancer. Now I see her wrapped in fuzzy footie pajamas with a contagious smile, convincing me she was fine even when I knew she was not. I do not remember the end anymore. I remember the middle. I remember her life.

This was not some magical process. I did not wake up one day and declare myself healed. I stumbled into it. I cried for years before I wrote a word. But eventually, I started waking up at 5:00 a.m. I started writing this book. I sat down every morning, with a mug of tea I rarely finished, and I returned to her. I relived it all. Not to torture myself but to honor her. I wrote to remember. I wrote because it was the only thing I knew how to do. I wrote for two hours, till my family woke up, every morning. I wrote through tears and over flashbacks, and slowly, my fingertips unknowingly built a map.

I wrote this entire memoir thinking no one would ever read it.

At first, I just wanted it to exist. For my family. For Mili and Emma. I wanted it to be real in the world, even if it never left my hard drive. But then something tugged at me. A quiet, persistent voice that said, "This matters." My story could help someone.

I did not know how to help people in grief. I just knew I had to. And then, the strangest thing happened. One day, maybe divine timing or maybe just Siri eavesdropping, I saw an ad to become a certified grief coach. It lit up in my mind, as though someone had taken a highlighter to my soul. That was it.

I signed up. I took the course. I devoured everything I could and I built a coaching business. I was not just healing, I was evolving. I was beginning to live in the space where pain met purpose. I was creating meaning. I was not telling anyone how to grieve. I was showing them through my story.

When you help others, you heal too.

I connected with Tom Zuba's second book, *Becoming Radiant*. A man who had lost both children and his wife, and yet, he was still standing. I thought, *If he can stand, so can I. And if I can stand, maybe someone else will believe they can too.*

And now, here you are. Reading this.

Maybe your grief is fresh. Maybe it is decades old but still pressing into your ribcage like it happened yesterday. Maybe you are barely surviving. Or maybe you are just beginning to consider that something else might be possible.

I want you to know that I have not forgotten the darkness. I have not "moved on" or "let go." I have integrated the pain. I have chosen to honor it, instead of being swallowed by it. And somehow, through the fog, I have found the light again.

It is not a straight path. There is no manual. There is only your breath, and your feet, and your choice to take one step forward, even if you have no idea where you are going.

Maybe I've always lived this way: moving fast, leaping forward before the wheels stopped spinning. It nearly cost me my voice once, back when I was three and crashing through the living room on that little yellow lion toy. I nearly bit my tongue off. But I survived, and my voice survived. And now, decades later, that same force–that wild, relentless spirit–carries me still. That same voice fights to be heard. Only now, it carries purpose too.

I now live in a place where I do not feel like I lost my daughter. I feel like I gained her, fully.

I carry her light and energy forward in everything I do. And my life is richer, deeper, and infinitely more meaningful because of her.

I never wanted this. But now I do not want to give it back.

This is the bridge I crossed. And now, I want to show you what lies on the other side.

Dear Addie, thank you for ... showing me that even when grief tried to silence my voice, your spirit became the bridge that carried me back to myself, unbroken and more alive than ever.

12

Evolution of a Miracle

"When you change the way you look at things,

the things you look at change."

−Wayne Dyer

There are stories that change your life, not just because they are heartbreaking or heroic, but because they mirror something inside of you that you had not yet named.

One of those stories came to me through a woman named Jeanette.

Her mother, Beverly, purchased my coaching sessions on her behalf. She was one of my first clients. Beverly wanted to help her daughter move forward in her grief, but Jeanette was stuck. Not the kind of stuck that looks like despair from the outside, but the quieter kind. The kind that lingers for years and builds a wall around your heart. The day her son Chase died, his thirteenth birthday, was the day she stopped telling their story. He had been hit by a car while crossing the street in their neighborhood. She could not move beyond the thought that it was preventable. That maybe he had made a mistake. That maybe she had. And so she carried that weight alone, wrapped in guilt, repeating the moment like it was her punishment.

When we began working together, I could see something in her. She had already built a beautiful legacy in her son's name. She was doing everything she could think of to honor him. But she could not speak his story without completely melting down. For years she had avoided saying his name out loud. For years she had been haunted by the question no grieving parent ever wants to hear, "How many children do you have?" She did not know what to say. Her body responded before her words could form. The answer never felt right. Either way, it hurt.

She was afraid to relive the story because she believed doing so would destroy her.

But I believe we have to relive the pain to reshape it, and she eventually did. Through a deep meditative process, we discovered the truth of what else that day could mean.

Chase was an organ donor. He saved several lives that day. A man. A young girl. People who now breathe and walk and dream because of him. Jeanette had made that decision in the depths of her despair. When the world was crashing around her, she gave that gift, his final act of generosity. And in doing so, she gave others life. That decision made Chase a hero.

Slowly, she began to see him that way too.

She practiced telling his story again. She cried. She paused. She tried again. She began to speak of him, not as a tragedy, but as someone who gave. Someone who still gives. She tells his story now with her chin up, not because the pain has gone away, but because her perspective has evolved. She still grieves, but now she also beams. She calls him her hero, and she means it with every cell in her body.

She still gets asked that dreaded question, "How many children do you have?" But now she answers it with pride.

"Three," she says. "One of them is in heaven." And then she tells them all about her hero named Chase.

Watching Jeanette reframe her story helped me articulate something I had felt for a long time, but could never quite put into words: Our healing is not about forgetting or even accepting, but rather about finding the courage to see the same story through a new lens.

Watching her evolve cracked something open in me. I saw with new eyes that the most painful stories can become the most powerful—not despite the pain, but because of it.

Who Am I?

I never expected one of the bravest moments of my life to become a lifeline for someone else. I spent most of my first Tony Robbins summit trying to disappear into the crowd. But something shifted in me when we were asked to declare a new identity. The old one, the one defined by hospitals, sorrow, and loss—had worn through. That night, I did something that scared me more than anything I had ever done in the military, fire academy, or delivery room: I wrote about who I was becoming through my grief, and posted it on his Facebook group.

It was deep into the night when I posted. My bedroom was dark except for the soft glow of my phone screen. My fingers hovered over the share button, trembling. Sharing my feelings publicly was a big step for me. I had reread the message more than a dozen times.

> My daughter died of cancer, now what ... who am I? Five years ago, I was totally numb with a fake smile on my face and tears in my heart, but thanks to a whole lot of soul searching and

hard work, I have completely transformed myself. I will keep growing in my grief, but for now I have a new purpose, and more clarity than ever before on how to help others. Years later, my smile is my truth and it's filled with pure appreciation for the gift I was given.

Every day is not perfect, and there are still moments of struggle, but now I have immense gratitude for the 3 years and 17 days my daughter was here with us that nobody can ever take away from me. Life truly is happening FOR me, not to me, and I have a lifetime of inspiration to prove it. I believe we all have the healing power inside us, we just have to find it and embrace the journey each day. Thank You Tony for helping me become deeply present in my life, be the best mother I can be, and grow into the person my daughter would be proud of. I am eternally grateful.

I finally hit "post," telling myself nobody would see it anyway. It was just a personal exercise buried inside a Facebook group. I needed to get it out. I did not expect it to echo back.

By morning, thousands of people had viewed it and responded with comments about how posting my new identity provided encouragement for them and how simply having more gratitude can play such a big role in healing from loss. I was humbled. My story impacted people worldwide who were struggling with grief, and that was heartwarming. I replied to as many people as I could.

A year later, someone from Tony's Facebook team personally reached out to me during the next summit. My post had somehow resurfaced. They said it moved them deeply. And then, they asked if I would be willing to speak directly with Tony—live—in front of over a million viewers.

I wanted to say no. I wanted to hide.

But I said yes.

With only minutes to prepare my thoughts, which is typically how Tony does things because he wants people to be in the moment and not rehearsed, I sat alone at the kitchen table in front of my computer. My heart was pounding through my chest, and I felt like I might pass out before I was called upon. When the moment came, I spoke from the part of me that still held Addie. I shared my gratitude for the way Tony's words had guided me out of the fog and back into my life, how I had transformed the day my daughter had died. And that now I valued raising my other daughters more than the pain of losing Addie.

He looked at me, paused, and said, "You have a beautiful soul."

And just like that, everything changed.

I felt a sense of confidence. A confirmation that I could *really* inspire others, even Tony himself, just by sharing my story.

I did not know it then, but a stranger in that virtual crowd would find me at another event years later. With tears welled up in his eyes, he told me that after hearing my story on the summit, he had come to a realization.

For the longest time, he believed the most painful season of his life was when his wife had cancer. But now, he saw it differently. He told me it was actually the season he was most proud of, because it was when he had been the most selfless. The most present. The most human. He had held her hand through it all. He had shown up when it counted. And now, that memory was no longer only a wound, it had become a badge of honor.

His words moved me so deeply, I struggled to accept them. I never know how to respond when someone tells me I helped them. I do not accept thanks easily. That is still something I am working on.

But moments like that remind me why I tell these stories, why I say the hard things out loud.

This chapter is not just about what happened to us.

It is about what we do next.

It is about the life we build afterward.

End of an Era

Retirement came quietly for me, like the closing of a well-worn book. In 2023, after twenty-two years of military service, plus four years before that in ROTC, and even more if you count my high school years in Civil Air Patrol, I took off the uniform for the last time.

I was not sad. There was no aching goodbye, no identity crisis. I had known for a while that chapter was ending, and I was ready. It was not the job that I would miss, it was the people. The ones who had shaped me. The ones I had mentored and led. The ones who knew what it meant to carry the mission quietly in the background.

I had considered skipping a retirement ceremony altogether, just walking out one day with a polite smile and a whispered "thank you." But something inside told me not to do that. I needed to mark the moment. I needed to show my daughters who their mother had been all those years. I needed to thank the people who had made this career what it was. I needed to close the book in a way that honored every chapter.

So I returned to where it had all begun, ROTC Detachment 105 at the University of Colorado, Boulder, and I stood at the front of that familiar room with my girls in the audience. They were only six and eight, but they were old enough to remember that moment. I hoped they would.

Instead of reciting the Air Force core values one last time, I shared my black sheep values, the ones I had quietly lived by all along. The ones that would guide me forward now that I was finally free to choose my own path. I was armed with a new kind of resilience, one I could only gain by leaving the service. Ashlie flew in from Hawaii, where the government had relocated her. She touched my heart deeply with her speech about the moments that built and defined our longstanding friendship. I had grieved the end of my career long before it came. And that day, I felt nothing but peace. It felt like a celebration of life.

But a moment that caught me off guard came from someone who had known me my whole life. My brother, Greg, stood up to speak. His words were humble, direct, and packed with the kind of truth you only share when you know your audience down to their core. He said I was his mentor, not just in uniform, but in life. And that was the point even my dad got emotional. That's how I knew Greg meant it.

We didn't talk much about our grief after Addie. Maybe I didn't make it easy. Maybe we didn't know how. But I felt his grief and his love in the way he showed up. At the ceremony, I overheard him telling a friend about his volunteer work with Angel Flight, flying patients like Addie to care they desperately needed. That's how I know she still matters to him, and that means everything to me.

Greg doesn't speak in grand gestures, but he acts with meaning. A few months before my ceremony, after his military retirement, he moved his family to Colorado. They bought a house just down the road from us and he accepted a job with United Airlines. Maybe one day he'll fly a child just like Addie to the North Pole for Christmas. We'll have to wait and see.

Our family doesn't always say the hard things out loud, but we show up in ways that speak louder. Through gestures. Through presence. Through choosing, again and again, to stay close, even when the world has tried to pull us apart. And in that room, surrounded by the people who shaped my past, I saw clearly who would walk with me into the future.

Santa Wishes

The year that followed retirement brought with it a quiet kind of joy. I built my grief coaching business. I poured energy into our nonprofit foundation for pediatric cancer research. I taught fitness classes at the gym. But what filled me most was the time I spent with my girls, the kind of time I used to crave in between those long duty days. Now I was there for all of it. I made space for the joy and was intentional about my time.

I watched Mili stick her first beam routine at her gymnastics meet and dance with open arms at an Andy Grammer concert. I watched Emma take the stage in her first theater production, her eyes wide with possibility. I brought home a new puppy, and their faces lit up in a way I will never forget. Those were the moments I used to dream about, and now I was living them. And I was fully present.

We made pizza on Fridays. We went back to Disney. We gave the girls YES days that they had earned, full of their wildest wishes. I was no longer surviving, I was living the life I had transformed.

But grief is not linear.

It does not follow the calendar or the milestones. It does not care if you are finally happy. It returns when you least expect it.

For me, December had become something promising. A month I used to dread had turned into one I looked forward to the most. We had created rituals: community service projects on Addie's birthday, holiday festivities, the gentle placement of her ornament on the tree, a visit to her grave on December 20th, where we would play "Let It Go" and dance together. It had taken years to get to that place, and I had arrived. December no longer broke me. It lifted me.

But this past year, something shifted.

The girls were quiet. The light in their eyes felt dimmer. They did not want to celebrate. They moved through the season like their shoes were too heavy. And then it happened.

We were parked at Sonic, getting our traditional tater tots in honor of Addie's birthday. It was supposed to be a moment of joy. A ritual that brought smiles. Instead, the girls started crying. And then I started crying.

But it was not the same kind of crying. This time, the pain was not mine alone. This time, I felt their pain, and it sliced through me in a way I was not prepared for.

Emma, now seven years old, said she did not know if she belonged in our family. Not because she was adopted, but because she was the only one who had never met Addie.

Mili, who seemed much older than nine some days, said she felt Addie's memory slipping away. That her connection with her was fading, and she did not know how to hold onto it.

Those words gutted me in a way only a mother can understand. The grief was layered. It was no longer just mine. It was theirs too.

And I had not seen it coming.

I had been so focused on honoring Addie's life. On teaching them how to celebrate her. I had not realized that my girls were still finding their own place in this story. Their grief did not match mine. How could it? We all grieve differently. And that December, their journey took a turn I had not prepared for.

The next morning, I found a letter Emma had written to Santa. In her careful handwriting, she asked for just one thing, "Can you please bring Addie back so I can meet her?" I stood there holding the note, tears rushing down my face, struck by the ache and innocence in that wish.

I wanted to say yes. I wanted to tell her there was still magic in the world, that somehow Santa might be able to grant the one wish even I couldn't. But instead, I sat beside her, pulled her into my lap, and said, "If Addie could come back, even for just a minute, I think she would tell you how proud she is to have you as a sister." Emma smiled, holding in her curious thoughts, and then snuggling up to me like a cub to her mama bear.

In that moment, I realized something—grief may never leave us, but neither does love. And sometimes, the miracles come, not in getting what we wish for, but in knowing how deeply we are all bonded together forever.

That night, I pulled out an old book we hadn't read in a while, *The Invisible String*. I bought it for Mili after Addie died. I used to read it to her often, especially in those early days when she was trying to understand how someone could be gone and their spirit still be with us, to let her know she still had an older sister. "No one is ever truly gone," I reminded her as we turned the pages. "There's always an invisible string, connecting us through love."

Mili silently looked up at me with her mature eyes full of wisdom, "Thank you for the reminder, Mom," and then she hugged me tighter than ever.

So I paused that December. We still did our community project for Addie's birthday, but I let go of the rest. I listened. I allowed space. I gave grace.

I questioned myself. *Did I cause this? Did I make them feel like they had to celebrate when they wanted to mourn?*

But I came back to this truth: our paths will never line up perfectly. Just like Cody and I in our journeys. Grief is not synchronized.

Everyone has their own timeline. Their own breaking point.

I believe they will rise. But I cannot force it.

All I can do is be there when they do.

That is my gift.

Addie's Song

Every year on January first, I sit down with a quiet mind and a hopeful heart. I scroll through my phone, letting the photos and videos trigger memories I might have forgotten. I write down every meaningful moment I can think of from the past year. The ones that made me laugh. The ones that taught me hard lessons. The ones that caught me off guard with beauty. I let the whole year wash over me, and I celebrate those memories because they are irreplaceable.

I want to be grateful for what was. I want to be present for what is. I want to reach for what could be. But I know that to do that, I have to start from where I am. I have to know the moment I am standing in.

Last year, I channeled my grief into a song I wrote for Addie. It was born in the middle of the night. I woke up, and the words just poured out of me, raw and real. I wanted to build something that honored her, even if I knew nothing about writing a song. I insisted on creating a melody using the notes A, D, and E. People thought I was a little bit crazy.

But I knew. I had no musical talents, but hearing music was a form of transcendence for me. And now, I could create.

I hired a young music teacher to help us. I brought the girls into it. Cody, too. I wrote the lyrics and we built the melody together. We practiced in the living room. We recorded it in the home office with a microphone in our hands. When the girls sang it, I cried tears of joy and grief wrapped together.

Addie was there. I could feel her.

And in that moment, I knew we had made something sacred.

> I carry you, on your journey, to be free
>
> I carry you, one day together, we will be
>
> You are my light, your heart beats on
>
> You make the world a better song
>
> Through pain and fears, I carry you
>
> Through all your tears, I carry you
>
> I … will carry you

Every day.

Addie is in my bones. In my breath. In my stubborn refusal to stay down. In my girls' laughter. In the moments I pause and notice the sunset. She is in the song, in the pages of this book, in every brave decision I make to keep living a life she would be proud of.

My Awakening

This chapter of my life has been one of quiet miracles. Of deep listening. Of slowing down.

Both sets of our parents celebrated their fiftieth wedding anniversaries this past year. They have now all lived eight years beyond losing their granddaughter. That truth is still difficult to say out loud without a pause. But it reminds me, in the most piercing way, that time is precious. That love, real love, lasts longer than we think it will. That presence matters. Addie taught us all that.

Several months ago, I said yes to a yoga and personal growth retreat. It was not the kind of thing I used to do. It's not typically where I found relaxation or answers, but yoga and mindfulness have grown on me throughout this journey. I have learned to calm my energy and seek a deeper connection with myself. So, I was open. I was curious. And I was evolving.

At the retreat, we had a sound bath ceremony. The kind where vibrations move through your body and bypass the logic in your brain. I was lying there, feeling the tones rise through my spine. I could see light from an orange and pink sunset beaming down on me, an undeniable sign of Addie's presence.

A speaker that day said something I could not shake. While she was sharing her inspiring story, four words she said caught me off guard—words I had heard before, but never paired together in a single thought: "change in perception" and "miracles." She used them in separate parts of her talk, unrelated, almost in passing. But for some reason, in my mind, they fused and spoke right to my soul. I circled the words in my notebook and stared at them. I let them tumble around in my head, over and over. *What if miracles coming true is not about changing outcomes, but about seeing things differently?*

And somewhere between the hum of the bowls, the bright colors in my mind, and the stillness of the room, I knew I had found it. How to close this chapter of my grief journey—the last story to conclude this book. It came through me like a current. Later I explained it to a group of women I had just met. And the moment I did, it became my truth.

I had always wished for a miracle. People had prayed relentlessly for Addie. For years, I thought the miracle would be her survival. I begged for it. I bargained for it. I wished on dandelions down to the last seed of hope. I lit candles and scoured every corner of the universe. But that is not the miracle I received.

Addie lives on. In all of us. And I survived.

Now, I am not just surviving. I am thriving.

I am living a life that was made more beautiful *because* of her. Because of who she was. Because of what she taught me. Because of what I refused to let die when she did.

That is my survival miracle. It did come true, just not in the way I expected.

Oftentimes I would visit this inner conflict in my mind. If Addie were still here, Emma would likely not be. But now, I have a more beautiful life because of both of them, and I would not change anything.

I used to think my stubbornness was a flaw. But now, I see it for what it is.

A gift.

A divine, unyielding force that refused to let me stay buried. The part of me that asked, "What now?" when it felt like the world had ended. The part that said, "There is more to this story." The part that insisted there had to be something *after* the pain.

I have learned not to listen to every voice society offers about grief. There are rules, yes, but they are not all meant for me. If I had followed them all, I would never have written this book. I would never have created a song. I would never have taught others how to stand again.

Many people stay stuck. Not because they want to, but because nobody showed them what it could look like to do otherwise. I want to be that someone. We are not meant to suffer forever. We are meant to learn from suffering and then rise. When you have the right tools, you can heal again.

You can live again.

You can let life crack you open, and you can become someone new—someone braver, someone more honest, someone who holds joy and sorrow in the same open palm.

That is what evolving in grief has meant for me. There is always a next chapter, until there is not.

And then, there is your legacy. If my daughter had a cancer that was one in a million, then that makes me one in a million as her mother.

So if you have something to say, something to write, something to give to the world, do it now. Do not wait for the right time. Because it is never going to feel like the right time, but it is always the right story.

Death is not the worst thing—not living is.

So now, let me show you how to find the life waiting for you.

Dear Addie, thank you for ... teaching me that my miracle was never about changing fate but in finding the courage to keep loving, keep living, and keep carrying you forward in every breath I take.

13

Rewritten Pathway

*"We choose to go to the moon in this decade and do the other things,
not because they are easy, but because they are hard."*

—JFK

When my daughter Addie took her last breath, the world as I knew it stopped. I was instantly thrust into a darkness so profound, I was unsure if I would ever see the light again.

Maybe you are there now, in that heavy, suffocating place of loss where hope feels impossibly distant. If you are, I want you to know one thing clearly—*you are not alone.*

Grief, I learned, does not follow neat guidelines or simple paths, yet there are gentle ways through it. I discovered, through many moments of despair and quiet breakthroughs, that we have the ability not only to survive significant loss, but also to rewrite our stories, to reshape our pain into purpose and our grief into gratitude. This process became my lifeline, my roadmap from anguish back to meaningful living.

Join me on this seven-step journey through grief to rewrite your story, or support someone who is rewriting theirs. Loss can be defined in many ways. It can be the death of a loved one or pet, divorce or loss of a relationship, a change in your health, or losing a job or financial security.

Grief is the most common, but also unique, human experience.

These steps loosely follow the known stages of grief and are deeply rooted in real moments from my own story, guiding you practically and compassionately toward your own rewriting. I will show you how to breathe again, to endure the intense bursts of grief, to ask questions bravely, reframe your painful experiences, integrate healing rituals, transform your relationship with grief, and ultimately, to evolve into the person you are meant to become.

Your story matters. Your healing is within reach. Let's R.E.W.R.I.T.E. your grief journey together and find out what your story can become. You do not need to believe it all right now. You just need to believe that it is *possible.* Because if I can do this, so can you.

This is your invitation, not to erase the past, but to reimagine the future. Not to silence your grief, but to write a new chapter alongside it. You have already survived the unimaginable. Now let me show you what else you can do.

STEP 1

Recover

"No act of kindness, no matter how small, is ever wasted."

–Aesop

When loss rips through your life, hopes and dreams are shattered and the ground beneath you disappears. Nothing feels real. Nothing feels safe. I have stood in that place—barely existing in a world that no longer made sense. My heart is here with yours.

Remember to breathe.

That was all I could do the moment Addie's tiny body lay motionless before me. It felt as though my own lungs had betrayed me. Each breath that I took was one she did not, a cruel reality that gripped my heart with unbearable anguish. My world had stopped spinning, yet somehow, inexplicably, I continued to breathe. I repeated it silently, my own quiet thought. *Breathe in, breathe out.* It was mechanical and desperate. Just one breath, then another. That was all I could manage, and that was OK.

The days following her death unfolded in a fog of disbelief, my mind clinging to impossible wishes. I remember hyperventilating, the room around me fading, my breath frantic and shallow. How could I inhale when my daughter could not? How was it fair for me to live, to breathe, to exist without her laughter echoing down the hallway or her tiny footsteps walking into my room at sunrise?

Give yourself grace.

In the initial stages of grief, you may feel denial and anger. There were days when numbness protected me, wrapping around my emotions like a thick blanket. Other moments brought waves of sharp, piercing pain so intense they left me gasping again. Some days you might feel compelled to fill every waking moment with busyness, desperate to outrun the silence and the absence. For me, it never mattered how fast or far I ran; grief was always there, patiently waiting.

I learned quickly, and painfully, that my grief was like my fingerprint: unique, complex, and completely mine. Whatever your response, know this: You are normal.

In grief, what we do isn't always guided by reason. For weeks after Addie died, her empty car seat remained fastened securely behind me in our minivan. Every morning, Mili would innocently ask when her sister was coming home, her words slicing through my heart each time. Still, I could not bring myself to remove the seat. I needed more time, even though each glance at that empty spot was an agonizing reminder of what was lost. There is no timeline for grief, no milestone you must reach by a certain date. It took weeks before I could release that small part of my daughter, and that was perfectly fine.

Give grace to others.

When Addie died, my imagined future vanished. There were no words of comfort adequate enough to soothe that reality. People tried, they truly did. Friends and family reached out, offering phrases meant to heal by saying, "At least you still have Mili," or "Addie is with the angels now." Each well-intended comment stung, despite the kindness behind it. I learned quickly that people often stumble awkwardly over grief because we rarely discuss death openly.

I wished deeply for understanding rather than comfort. I yearned to hear, "My favorite memory of Addie is …" or "I think about Addie and your family often." Those heartfelt connections, those stories, helped shift my focus away from the overwhelming emptiness to the meaningful life my daughter lived, if only for a moment.

When people wrote messages of love, their thoughtfulness brought precious comfort.

A friend said, "In three years and seventeen days, Addie touched more lives than most people do in a lifetime. She taught us lessons on bravery and endurance, but most of all, Addie, Mili and their parents showed us an incredible story of love, and how love always triumphs. Thank you for the privilege of letting us accompany you during this past year. We will carry Addie in our hearts forever."

Those messages showed me, if only briefly, a glimmer of purpose behind Addie's life and death. They reminded me that connection could gently illuminate even the darkest places. I appreciated them very much.

Reach out to someone who has walked your path.

The day after my daughter died, I contacted the wife of one of Cody's fighter pilot friends. Their son had passed away from cancer a few years prior. I had never met her or heard their story, yet instantly we shared an unspoken bond no one else around me understood. Finding a connection can help you survive grief's loneliness.

Our call did not lessen my grief, but it softened my isolation, reassuring me that even in the deepest darkness, I was not alone.

You are not alone either. Right now, in this moment, breathing might be your only task, your only accomplishment, and that is enough. Breathe in, breathe out. Allow yourself grace. Extend it to others, and begin to feel a gentle, compassionate hope rising within. Your grief journey is terrifying and overwhelming, but within this pain lies a quiet message.

You have survived today, and that is the bravest start.

Carry This With You

Step 1: Recover

- Remember to breathe.
- Give yourself grace.
- Give grace to others.
- Reach out to someone who has walked your path.

STEP 2

Endure

"Although the world is full of suffering,
it is also full of the overcoming of it."

—Helen Keller

If you're staring at the numbness or sitting in the silence after a goodbye or even if you are angry—here's what I can tell you: You don't have to rush to feel better. You don't have to be "strong" in the way people often define it. Sometimes strength is simply letting life in.

Here's the thing about heartbreak: It doesn't just shatter you. It reshapes you. It tears apart the old framework of your life and slowly, painfully, builds something new. Not better. Not worse. Just ... different.

There's something profoundly disorienting about numbness and denial. It's not what people expect when they imagine grief. Most think it's about tears, and yes, there are those, too, but my numbness was heavier. More suffocating. It showed up quietly, like fog rolling in after a long night, and before I even realized it was there, grief swallowed me whole.

In those first months after Addie died, I wasn't living; I was floating. Conversations happened around me. Holidays came and went. Mili smiled at me with all her light, and I smiled back, but I couldn't feel the warmth behind my own expression. I was there, but I wasn't. The photos from that time show a functioning mom. But I know how broken I was inside.

Grief isn't linear.

It loops, it spirals, it hides behind joy and jumps out on sunny days when you least expect it. There were moments when I found comfort in my community and other moments when I wanted to isolate completely. There were days I could function, and days when brushing my teeth felt like a huge accomplishment. I have learned that both are normal.

One of the hardest things I grappled with was this inner contradiction. I was still Addie's mom, yet she wasn't here. And I had Mili, this beautiful child who needed me fully, and I couldn't give her everything she deserved in those first months. That was one of the sharpest edges of my grief: the guilt of surviving. Of still being a mom, and not *feeling* like one.

Maybe you are there, too, gripped by depression, unsure if you will ever recover. I promise you this: It is possible to want to live again, even after the worst thing has happened. You just need a place to begin.

There's no *right* way to grieve. There is only your way.

Sometimes it's writing a thank-you card when you can't speak. Sometimes it's letting yourself completely fall apart during a weightless bed experience with no one watching. Sometimes it's crying in the parking lot of Target when you hear a song on the radio. And sometimes it's saying yes to a dance performance that may be about your own soul searching.

For me, grief meant doing. For someone else, it might mean resting. Sleeping. Screaming. Walking until their feet blister. Sitting in a quiet church pew. Turning to faith. Turning away from it. Taking the next breath without understanding how. All of it counts.

You don't have to be healed to begin creating a legacy. A small act of creation, in the middle of devastation, was a soft pulse that reminded me I was still here. And maybe, just maybe, Addie was too.

Helping future children with cancer felt like forward motion for me. I didn't sit on the couch and cry all day, and that became another layer of guilt, because people expect visible grief. But for me, the pain was buried beneath to-do lists, grant applications, and late-night research about cancer mutations.

To anyone burdened by the invisible weight of grief, healing is not about forgetting or moving past the memories. It's about embracing the reality of loss, allowing emotions their rightful place, and letting grief flow naturally through your life without judgment or resistance. The path to healing is not straightforward. It's filled with unexpected moments of discomfort, pain, and release. But when we courageously allow ourselves to feel it all, we open doors to true emotional freedom.

Give yourself permission to let the "grief bursts" happen.

It's normal to be overcome by an emotion that feels like a seizure. These bursts can provide a connection you may not even imagine. When I see a child, bald from cancer treatments, tears pour from my eyes, yet my heart smiles and explodes with joy at the same time. I can feel Addie's presence beside me.

Each moment spent honoring your pain brings you one step closer to understanding yourself better, loving yourself deeper, and living with a heart more open than ever before.

This realization became not just a lesson for me, but a guiding truth I now eagerly share.

Most people just endure the suffering and never figure out how to get to the next phase. Some stay there the rest of their life. They tell themselves that it will always be painful.

But what if you didn't say that?

Carry This With You

Step 2: Endure

- Grief isn't linear.
- There is no right way to grieve. There is only your way.
- Give yourself permission to let the "grief bursts" happen.

STEP 3

Wonder

When I was caring for Addie, I never thought, "What if she doesn't survive?" because I always thought, "What if she does?" I knew she would. I needed to think that way to be the best mother I could be to her.

A curious mindset was ingrained in me from a young age. By challenging myself with questions, I have survived and thrived both in the armed forces and through my daughter dying of cancer. I have built up my resilience for my next challenges in life, especially the ones I don't see coming.

Healing doesn't come from arriving at a destination. It comes from having the courage to keep showing up in the middle of it all, with your tears, your questions, your trembling voice, and saying, *I'm still here.*

Sometimes, the right questions don't come in the form we expect. They arrive messy, uninvited, wrapped in discomfort. They demand honesty. But within that honesty is the seed of healing.

Some days, I would ask myself, *What am I doing here? What am I still holding on for? Can I survive this?*

On another day I would ask myself, *What does it mean to live after loss? What does presence look like now? How do I honor my daughter without losing myself?*

I didn't find all the answers right away, but asking these questions gave me direction when I had none. They grounded me. They reminded me that curiosity, especially about our own pain, isn't weakness. It's courage.

Convert your fear into curiosity and hope, then ask yourself: What if?

Grief has a way of turning everything you thought you understood inside out. During the workshops I took, the ones meant to rebuild my marriage or help me rediscover myself, I wasn't just carrying sorrow. I was carrying the wreckage of a life that no longer existed, while trying to figure out who I was in the one I had been unwillingly handed.

What if grief is not a weakness but my greatest gift? What does that look like?

What if Addie's memory isn't fading, but changing shape?

What if I'm not meant to go back to who I was before, but forward into someone newly defined?

I believe that sometimes healing doesn't start with answers. It starts with brave, painful questions.

What storms have you survived, and how have they shaped who you are becoming?

I never imagined the day would come when I would pull my own steering wheel toward destruction, yearning desperately to feel something, anything, beyond the numbness of my grief. When you lose a child, the world transforms into a place that feels empty and foreign, each innocent question about motherhood becoming a cruel reminder of the life you had and lost. My life was cracking silently beneath a veil of forced smiles and social pleasantries. I bargained relentlessly with reality, hoping to reverse time, overwhelmed by a heartache so inconceivable it felt impossible to bear.

Yet, in that terrifying skid off the highway, I found something unexpected. Clarity came crashing through in my darkest hour, revealing the depth of my despair and igniting a fragile spark of hope within the chaos. That spark whispered softly, "You are meant for more than this moment."

In the pain of that truth, I discovered a raw understanding that surviving grief is not just enduring the storm but learning to embrace life through the pouring rain.

The path forward begins in the quiet bravery of reflection, and though the answers may feel distant, the questions themselves may be enough to guide you to your next step.

I recently read a book from one of my favorite authors, Rachel Hollis. She's real, raw, and writes about life in a way I truly connect with. Her books make me laugh and smile inside, as so much of her experience rings true for me. In her latest book, *What if YOU Are the Answer?* right in the introduction, she states, "So, my friend, I'm no longer looking for answers; I'm looking for wisdom."[2] What if we all looked for something beyond the answer? What if we all sought out a way to understand life, to experience it in a new way?

There is a quiet kind of courage in asking the hard questions, the ones that make your stomach drop and your mind go still. In the death class, it was not the answers that changed me. It was the questions.

Who would raise our children if we died tomorrow? What words have I left unsaid? What would I want my final moments to look like? Who would I want holding my hand?

These were not abstract hypotheticals. They were intimate, soul-searching invitations to look at life through the lens of death, not with fear, but with clarity. I learned that asking these questions is not morbid. It is liberating. It is not about preparing for death; it is about preparing to live. Fully. Boldly. Without apology.

When we dare to ask ourselves what truly matters, we begin to live with intention. We let go of the noise, the clutter, the pressure to perform. We come back to our values. We see our relationships with fresh eyes. We soften. We forgive. We plan, not out of fear, but out of love.

The questions from that death class still echo in my mind, not as burdens, but as guideposts. They remind me that I am not here forever, but I am here now. And that, perhaps, leads us to the most important question of all.

What will you do with your now?

In grief, there are no roadmaps. But questions are like trail markers—they don't always show you the full path, but they remind you to keep walking.

And when you let them in, really let them in, without demanding resolution, you begin to understand. You begin to see that grief isn't just about pain—it's about love, and transformation, and the aching beauty of what it means to *have had* something, someone, that mattered enough to break you.

What comes next is not easy. But it just might change everything.

> ## Carry This With You
>
> <u>Step 3: Wonder</u>
>
> - Convert your fear into curiosity and hope, then ask yourself: What if?
> - What storms have you survived, and how have they shaped who you are becoming?
> - What will you do with your now?

STEP 4

Reframe

"Life can only be understood backwards;
but it must be lived forwards."

—Søren Kierkegaard

What if the worst moment of your life held the very key to your healing?

Your grief deserves a second look. So do your regrets. The moment you cannot let go of might be the one that, when reframed, gives you the freedom you have been aching for.

Be open to transforming your thoughts.

I invite you to change the way you think about the past. Francis Weller, a psychotherapist, writer, and soul activist, said in his enlightening book, *The Wild Edge of Sorrow*, that "If you don't go there, you'll never return."[3] Taking action based on this statement has been the cornerstone of my journey.

What would it look like to revisit your most painful moment, not to suffer, but to search?

What might you find if you allowed yourself to reenter the scene and look for the love that was always there?

Can you give yourself permission to rewrite that moment, not as a tragedy alone, but as a testament to your love and your strength?

I believe if we focus on what we have lost, we can never fully appreciate what we have. You will not forget them. But you *can* let go of the weight that is keeping you stuck.

And when you do, you will not just survive your loss.

You will thrive.

You will breathe without guilt.

You will remember without pain.

And you will honor their life by fully living yours.

But first, you must change at your core.

There was a time when I thought vulnerability would cost me my credibility. That showing emotion, especially in a military leadership role, would somehow diminish the respect I had worked so hard to earn. I thought being strong meant holding it together. Stoicism was my armor, and grief felt like a crack in that foundation.

But I learned that vulnerability is not weakness. It is presence. It is being real in a world that so often demands we pretend.

When I finally shared my story with my team, when I spoke my daughter's name and allowed others to see the pain I carried, I was met with compassion, not discomfort. I was met with humanity, not judgment. And most surprisingly, I was met with connection.

Our office became a place where people no longer had to leave parts of themselves at the door. And it started because I stopped leaving mine behind. Vulnerability needs an invitation. Someone has to go first.

So if you are wondering how to begin, start with one truth. One sentence. One small window into what you are carrying. You do not have to bleed in front of everyone to be real. You just have to be honest.

Say one thing that you have been holding back.

You do not have to share every detail, but let people see something true about you. When you do, you are not only offering a part of yourself, you are creating space for someone else to do the same.

Grief taught me that people are not looking for perfect leaders. They are looking for human ones. The kind who show up, not in spite of what they have been through but because of it.

If you are reading this and holding something heavy, you do not have to carry it in silence. Start small. Say something true. See what happens next. *Sharing is caring.* Emma taught me that. And now I know, sharing is also healing.

Maybe you are holding a grief that feels impossible to carry. Maybe you are reading this, not because you want to but because you need something—even if you do not know what that something is yet.

I did not know I was searching for a safety net until I found one. Sitting in the back of that cancer conference where Brant spoke, I was still trying to claw my way back to myself. What he said that day about black sheep values did not fix everything, but it helped me begin again. It helped me reframe.

Your black sheep values are the core of who you are. They are not aspirational, they are foundational. They do not change just because life has. They are the parts of you that remain when everything else is stripped away. If you are lost, start there.

Start with one small act each day that reflects what matters to you.

Maybe it is a walk with someone you love. Maybe it is five minutes of stillness. Maybe it is standing up for something you believe in. You do not have to do it perfectly. You just have to begin.

Years later, I learned that Brant's son, Theo, had passed away during the pandemic. The grief I had struggled with the day I sat in the audience had finally come for him too. I reached out with a message. I told him the truth, that his book changed me. That his story was a light in the dark. That I was still here, living into my values. I wanted to give him hope. Because *hope* was one of his values. So was *impact*. And his theory had not just impacted me, it had saved me on days I did not even realize I was drowning.

He wrote back, which meant everything to me. Because connection is one of my values and that moment reminded me how we are never really alone in our pain, even when it feels like we are. We shared common ground: two parents walking parallel roads that finally intersected in the most unexpected way. I was just a few years ahead. I could offer him the one thing I had not had enough of back then: proof that it was possible to live again.

It's why I decided to write this book. For impact. For connection. For family. And for perseverance to reach the endless thread of gratitude that somehow still winds its way through my days. To help you, if you are ready, find your values and let them lead you home.

I believe in miracles. And this moment, this connection, was part of mine.

Now, maybe, it can be part of yours too.

Carry This With You

<u>Step 4: Reframe</u>

- ❯ Be open to transforming your thoughts.
- ❯ Say one thing that you have been holding back.
- ❯ Start with one small act each day that reflects what matters to you.

STEP 5

Integrate

"Some people want it to happen, some wish it would happen, others make it happen."

—Michael Jordan

Grief taught me that healing is not about one big moment of clarity. It is about tiny practices, repeated daily, until they start to feel genuine. Sometimes we look for the grand gesture, the sudden transformation. But what saved me were the smallest choices I made every day; the choices anchored me in the present, even when my heart was living in the past.

I never set out to become someone who meditated before sunrise, ran for miles without a goal, or found meaning in the placement of ink on skin. But when the ground fell out from under me, I had no choice but to build a new one beneath my feet. And I had to do it with the simplest materials I had: my breath, my steps, my memories, and my intention.

It started with the tattoo. One image. One name. A place to focus my aching love. Then came the running. Not because I liked it, but because it gave me a container for my pain. It gave me a start and a finish, and sometimes that was the only thing I could count on. Eventually, I found my way into stillness. Into priming. Into the quiet moments before the world wakes up when I could whisper to myself that I was still here.

Intentional living does not have to be elaborate.

You do not have to run marathons or meditate for hours. You just need to choose one thing. One habit that makes you feel a little more like yourself. Maybe it is drinking your coffee slowly. Maybe it is walking around your neighborhood without your phone. Maybe it is sitting on your porch and listening to the wind. And maybe, just maybe, it is deciding to remember joy.

The habits that helped me most were not complicated. They were consistent. I showed up for them, even on the days I did not want to. Especially on those days. And over time, those practices gave me back a sense of self. They reminded me that while grief would always live beside me, it did not have to lead.

One of the most pivotal shifts in my grief journey came from something I read in *Option B*, by Sheryl Sandberg and Adam Grant. In this book, Sheryl, the former CEO of Facebook, bravely writes about the sudden death of her husband, Dave, and how it permanently changed her life. She references a concept that I found to be extremely helpful in processing grief. She cites psychologist Martin Seligman in his well-known theory of the three P's—personal, pervasive, and permanent—and how they shape our response to trauma and loss.[4]

Let go of any misplaced guilt.

At first, my grief felt like it belonged to me alone, like I had failed Addie in some way, but my daughter's death wasn't a punishment, and it wasn't my fault. It wasn't *personal*. Letting go of that guilt was the first step toward compassion, for her and for myself.

Grief does not ruin every part of life.

Grief tries to convince us that everything is broken, that every corner of life is ruined. That's the lie of *pervasiveness*. And it's not true. Yes, one part of my world shattered, but not all of it. I still had children who needed me, love that surrounded me, and breath in my lungs. Grief could touch my life, but it didn't get to define it.

Sometimes the smallest practices can shift everything. Try keeping a gratitude journal—write down even the tiniest sparks of goodness. You may find those moments become anchors, pulling you back toward life.

The pain of grief is temporary.

For a long time, I believed the pain would never end. That this sharp, aching absence would be my forever. But even that has softened. That's what I learned about *permanence*—it's an illusion. The pain is temporary, but the love lasts forever.

Those three truths from *Option B* didn't erase my sorrow, but they helped me carry it differently. With less shame. With more grace.

This story, my story, is not a prescription. It is a possibility. A way of showing you that integration is not about doing everything, it is about doing something. It is about choosing to meet your pain with presence. To build a life that includes what you lost and honors what remains.

I used to think the goal was to move on. Now I know it is to move with your grief. And if there is one thing I hope you take from this, it is that you do not need to feel ready. You may never feel ready. You only need to begin. So ask yourself,

What small thing can I do today that brings me back to myself?

Then do it again tomorrow.

Carry This With You

Step 5: Integrate

- Intentional living does not have to be elaborate.
- Let go of any misplaced guilt.
- Grief does not ruin every part of your life.
- The pain of grief is temporary.

STEP 6

Transform

"Live life, don't let life live you."

−Pitbull

The words we say to ourselves matter. The thoughts we choose, even when they feel impossible to believe, can shape what comes next. I used to think healing would arrive with time, but it was never time alone. It was what I did with the time. What I whispered to myself on the days I could barely rise. What I wrote when no one else was reading. What I believed even when my heart said otherwise.

Transformation did not happen all at once. It happened in moments. Quiet moments. Raw, unremarkable moments. A shift in thought here. A change in language there. A choice to respond differently when someone said something well-meaninged but painful.

When someone said, "I cannot imagine anything worse than losing a child," I would freeze.

Now, I respond. Calmly. Clearly. With the voice of someone who has lived it and kept going. "I can imagine worse. A life without her would be worse. A life where I gave up afterward would be worse." That response is not rehearsed, it is lived. That is what I want people to understand.

The story of my grief was not meant to stay stuck in a chapter labeled "pain." It had more pages to write. It had a new language to find. And if you are reading this, yours does too.

You can let go of the pain.

You are grieving deeply because you loved deeply. You must now connect with your loved one differently. Here are some suggestions for continuing the bond with your loved one in a new way: Include something that represents your loved one in family photos or holiday cards. Seek out places and situations where you feel the presence of that person. Set aside time to journal about how this person has enhanced your life.

Contemplating thoughts, words, and quotes became my daily practice. When I learned to shift from "Why her?" to "Thank God for her," everything changed. Not all at once, but eventually. Slowly. With effort. With tears. With grace.

If you are lost in grief, I want you to know this: It is possible to transform it. Not erase it. Not forget it. But to shape it into something you can live with. Something that might one day even offer you peace.

Don't let grief be the end of your story.

Let it be the beginning of the bridge you build, step by step, into the life that is still calling your name.

David Kessler, author of four grief books and widely known as a world expert in the field, wrote a book titled *Finding Meaning*.

In it, he explains, "Like all the other stages, the sixth stage of grief requires movement. We can't move into the future without leaving the past. We have to say goodbye to the life we had and say yes to the future."[5]

The concept surrounding the sixth stage of grief is one that most people don't know and most never reach. It is not about healing. It is not even about peace.

It is about creating meaning.

Creating meaning doesn't end the grief. It transforms it into a life that still holds them, a life that is worthy of both your love and your survival. And in that life, they do not fade–they simply change the way they live on.

Carry This With You

Step 6: Transform

- You can let go of the pain.
- Don't let grief be the end of your story.
- The sixth stage of grief is about creating meaning.

STEP 7

Evolve

"The purpose of life is to discover your gift. The work of life is to develop it. The meaning of life is to give your gift away."

—David Viscott

Transformation is not a one-time event, it's a thousand small decisions. It is the choice to get out of bed, even when it hurts. It is the decision to speak your loved one's name, even when your voice shakes. It is allowing yourself to cry at Sonic on a Tuesday in December. It is honoring your sadness and your joy in the same breath.

You are meant to *learn* from the ache. To *become* something more honest, more human, more deeply present in the one and only life you have.

You can live with it—not in spite of it, not instead of it, but *with* it. You can carry your pain and still dance in the kitchen. You can ache and still laugh. You can cry and still create. You can remember and still imagine a future worth living.

This book has been part of my journey for a while now. I wrote it four years ago, but it was not time to publish it. I thought maybe it was only for my girls. That maybe nobody else would read it. But the truth was, I was still living the story. Still learning the lessons. Still evolving into the person who could write the ending with clarity and peace.

This book is not just about Addie, or grief, or cancer, or motherhood, or the moments that cracked me open. It is about what comes after. It is about the part nobody prepares you for: the rebuilding, the remembering, the choosing to live again.

Live in a way that honors what was lost, along with what remains.

Cody and I aren't the same people who met at that wedding all those years ago. What we didn't know back then is that love isn't forged in flirtation or clever banter. It's built in hospital rooms and middle-of-the-night medication alarms. It's made in silent blessings and awkward car rides. It's made when you stand beside someone who is shattered and you don't try to fix them, you just stay.

There were times our grief pulled us into different orbits. I retreated inward. He exploded outward. We fought for control in a world that offered none. We didn't always see eye to eye. Sometimes we didn't even recognize each other. But we never stopped choosing each other. Even when it was hard—especially when it was hard.

We lost our daughter, but we refused to lose our marriage. And maybe that's one of the quiet victories we don't celebrate enough. We're still standing. Not because it's easy. But because we remember who we were when we met, and we know who we've become since.

You are not broken beyond repair, you are unfinished.

This book is the story of how I found my way to that truth. It is a mirror and a map. It's a reminder that healing is possible. That you can live a meaningful, beautiful, connected life after devastation.

You are allowed to want more.

You are allowed to climb out.

You are allowed to carry your love forward without letting it consume you.

I hope this story showed you what is possible, not because I told you, but because you *felt* it. Because maybe you saw yourself in these pages, and something inside of you whispered, "I can too."

And if that voice is faint right now, that is OK. You do not have to know what your next chapter is yet. You just have to believe there is one. Let this book be your invitation. Let it be your permission. Let it be the reminder that death is not the worst thing—not living is.

And you are still here.

Carry This With You

Step 7: Evolve

- Live in a way that honors what was lost, along with what remains.
- You are not broken beyond repair, you are unfinished.
- You are allowed to want more.
- You are still here.

Epilogue

This is Cody writing—Christina's fighter pilot husband who was confident that the Anti-G Straining Maneuver taught to me by the US Air Force for flying jets was a fine substitute for Lamaze training in the delivery room.

I don't have the same memories from Addie's life, nor her death, as Christina does. We were there, together, for almost every moment. Yet the perspective was certainly different. After her passing, we went through emotions and withdrawals completely opposite from each other. As I left the military, a very strange thing started taking over my reality: Intense combat experiences started flashing back at seemingly random times. A particular civilian casualty incident, which happened three years before Addie was even born, started replaying like I was there again.

While I watched Christina struggle, and successfully begin to transform her grief, I was flailing, and I knew deep down that I had lost my purpose. The truth was, the same feeling from that moment gone wrong in combat was crowding against what I was hanging onto from the night of Addie's passing—it was shame. The shame I felt was not that I had done something wrong, it was that I couldn't do enough. I couldn't save those people. I couldn't solve the puzzle of my daughter's disease. I couldn't protect my family.

I have great respect for those trying to rebuild, and I recognize now how resistant to change I was in my own life. Christina swims in activity and used to shun the quiet time. I felt overwhelmed by the pace of work and family life, and desperately sought serenity and calmness. We both tended toward what was easy, what seemed comfortable. When I apply the Rewritten Pathway to my own life, I find it's the uncomfortable things which bring me the most growth. Christina has taught me so much—sometimes intentionally and sometimes through osmosis. I know that we are forming a new relationship as we discover ourselves, which is stronger than any I could imagine.

I'm fortunate to have a partner in marriage, who patiently let me walk my own path while clearly seeing I needed help. From the first day after Addie passed, I wondered when an entire day would go by without me thinking about and remembering her vividly. I feared letting her go. I feared it would be even more of a betrayal than not saving her. My pain was my connection to her, and if Christina has taught me anything, it's that grace comes first, then progress needs to follow. I know now that the pain in Addie's treatment, and eventually her death, was temporary. What remains is what I want: the glowing memory of a beautiful soul who made me the man I am today and inspires me toward a new version of myself with renewed purpose.

My new foundation, the better version of me I'm working toward, is based on Addie's spirit, Christina's love, and my daughters Mili and Emma.

A Final Note

Dear Reader,

From the depths of my heart, thank you for traveling through these pages with me, for allowing me to tell the story of my daughter and of the woman I became in the quiet echo of her absence.

Writing this book has been one of the hardest things I have ever done. Not because the words would not come. They came, in waves, in whispers, in the raw, jagged edges of memory. They came in the quiet hours when the house was still, and in the loud moments when grief knocked again. But because each time I sat down to write, I had to walk back into the fire.

I hope somewhere in these words you have found a small glimmer of comfort or perhaps just the reassurance that even in your darkest hours, you are not alone. My wish is that you will keep choosing to live fully, even when it hurts. That you will keep seeking the light that still waits for you beyond the edges of your sorrow.

If you feel ready to keep walking forward, to transform your grief, I have created *The Rewritten Pathway Reflection Guide* for you—a free workbook and journal drawn from the same steps that helped me survive and grow. You can find it at graduategrief.com. I invite you to join my community, where I continue to share tools, stories, and gentle reminders that healing remains possible.

If this book has brought you hope and inspiration, please pass it along to someone else who might still be searching. And if you feel moved, leaving a review on Amazon helps other grieving hearts discover these words precisely when they need them most.

In the space between grief and possibility—I Carry You.

With love and gratitude,

Christina

Acknowledgements

Perhaps more difficult than piecing this book together has been the quiet torment of deciding whose names belong on these pages. The truth is, I have lost far too much sleep worrying about who I might leave out. If you have lived this story beside our family, please know that your place is etched permanently in my heart, even if your name does not find itself here.

To my family:

Cody, thank you for allowing me to share Addie's story, for standing beside me through nights that felt endless, and for loving me when I could hardly recognize myself.

Mili and Emma, you are my most treasured gifts in this life. I love you more than words can ever say. Thank you for giving Mommy the time to finish this book.

Mom and Dad, you have stood beside me through every storm, every move, and every moment when I doubted if I could keep going. Your steadfast love and support have been the quiet force that held me together. I am who I am because of you.

Greg, Cristy, Collin, and Brie, thank you for always being by our side and staying close, even when we were miles apart.

JoMama and Papa Deaux, thank you for opening your home without hesitation and for reintroducing toddlers into your life.

To my extended New York family, thank you for giving us your time, your presence, and your love when we needed it most. Aunt Ro and Uncle Ron, thank you for inviting Addie to be buried with Alex. There are no words to hold the weight of that gift. Teeny (Elsa), thank you for designing Addie's exquisite foundation logo, a symbol that carries her spirit into the world. Dan, thank you for dressing up like a Minion, simply to make Addie and me smile. Dominique, thank you for crafting a beautiful Mickey Minion cake that made Addie's day. Aunt Marianne and Uncle Kevin, thank you for making memories on Mt. Evans with us.

To my truest friends:

Becks, Erica, Ashlie, Suzie, Anduin, Nichelle, Joylyn, and Bridget—thank you for staying close, especially when the road was hard. You have carried me through my career, through Addie's cancer, and through the fragile aftermath of grief. That means everything to me.

To those whose kindness and support have carried me further than they may ever know:

Our Air Force network of friends, thank you for showing up with meals and for continuing to stand with us as we pursue the mission of pediatric cancer research. My COANG COVID team, thank you for taking care of me as much as I did you.

Alan and Cheryl, thank you for being the best Alaskan neighbors anyone could wish for.

Andi and Sam, thank you for always stopping by on December 20th with baked goods.

Tahverlee, thank you for bestowing upon me the title of "way-shower" long before I knew what that truly meant for me.

Erin, thank you for putting your heart and soul into a beautiful retreat that motivated me to find the ending of this book.

KMo, thank you for your personal guidance and all the work you do to help veterans.

Amanda, thank you for helping us bring Addie's song to life.

Lynn, thank you for capturing our favorite black and white photo of Addie, a moment I hold closest to my heart.

Alie, thank you for the most memorable photo shoot I never wanted and am now the most grateful for. Addie's swing photo is a gift I cherish.

Amber, thank you for beautifully capturing the hope and joy in our family as we are now.

Mark, thank you for letting Addie come to Great Play whenever she felt well. The memories we have from there will live on forever.

Children's Hospital Colorado staff, thank you for your patience when I was not myself, especially Grant, Flori, Suzanne, Dr. Greffe, Dr. Faulk, and Dr. Roach.

Make-A-Wish, thank you for helping me even when I was too stubborn to admit I needed it.

Thank you to everyone who trusted me to share their stories and their names within these pages.

**To the people whose presence reminded
me I never had to walk alone:**

Erin, thank you for going first. Your memoir about Sam is beautiful and became my inspiration.

Rachael, thank you for giving me the gift of living my life without the fear of death. Henry's light shines bright in every fox I see.

Mary, thank you for giving me the gift of presence in my grief journey, reminding me to dance with my grief, even when it felt impossible.

Kim, thank you for sharing Arden's story with me and listening when nobody else could understand my feelings deep inside.

Kelly, at the Mike Bamford Foundation, thank you for transforming Addie's fingerprint into a keepsake necklace I will always hold dear.

Joan, at The Morgan Adams Foundation, thank you for nine years of guidance and mentorship in the nonprofit world.

Katie, thank you for your mentorship and for sharing the revelations of your grief journey with me. It has been my privilege to witness your transformation.

To the people who believed in me:

Zach, thank you for your remarkable work capturing my story for the Tony Robbins audience. Thank you for seeing who I was becoming, even before I could see it myself. Your belief helped me step into my own light.

Tony Robbins, thank you for transforming my life and for believing in me as a coach.

Dora, thank you for teaching me how to use my story to help others and for giving me the courage to step forward as a grief educator.

To all the podcast hosts who have given me space to share Addie's story so others might feel less alone–thank you.

To our foundation supporters:

Charles, thank you for believing in Hepatoblastoma research and for your courage in tackling the hardest problems.

Mike, thank you for your generosity, your partnership, and your belief in our mission to change the landscape of pediatric cancer research.

Norm, thank you for designing such inspirational artwork for Addie's t-shirts, helping to share her light with the world.

To all our family, friends, and those who believe in our mission, thank you for your unwavering support through the past nine years. We could not have raised over seven hundred thousand dollars for Hepatoblastoma research without you. I know we are headed toward the million mark in the coming years! Everyone who supports us carries a piece of her story into the world, and for that, I am honored.

Susan and the Arctic Explorers Preschool staff, thank you for your annual event in honor of Addie–for remembering her and for keeping her spirit alive, year after year. It means the world to us.

And to my dearest Adelaide ... you have given me more than I could ever give to you. For that, I am eternally grateful.

References

1. Tom Zuba, *Permission To Mourn* (Bish Press, 2015) p. 36.

2. Rachel Hollis, *What if YOU Are the Answer?* (Authors Equity, 2025) p. Xiii.

3. Francis Weller, *The Wild Edge of Sorrow* (North Atlantic Books, 2015) p. 107.

4. Sheryl Sandberg and Adam Grant, *Option B* (Penguin Random House, 2017) p. 16.

5. David Kessler, *Finding Meaning* (Scribner, 2020) p. 249.

About the Author

Photo Credit: Amber Braun

Christina Stiverson is a certified grief coach, retired US Air Force officer, fitness professional, and the president of Foundation for Addie's Research. Christina became passionate about rare pediatric cancer research and helping others through grief after her three-year-old daughter passed away in 2016. Her transformational story captured the hearts of millions when she was featured by Tony Robbins on his Time to Rise Summit. Amidst her volunteer work and coaching business, Christina finds immense joy in her life as a wife and mother to her three beautiful girls.

www.ingramcontent.com/pod-product-compliance
Lightning Source LLC
Chambersburg PA
CBHW032017150726
47990CB00005B/2002